The National Curriculum and its Assessment:

Final Report

Ron Dearing
December 1993

Chairman: Sir Ron Dearing
Chief Executive: Chris Woodhead

School Curriculum and Assessment Authority
Newcombe House
45 Notting Hill Gate
London
W11 3JB

Tel: 071 229 1234

CONTENTS

School Curriculum and Assessment Authority
Newcombe House, 45 Notting Hill Gate
London W11 3JB

Telephone: 071-243 9273
Fax: 071-243 1060

From the Chairman
Sir Ron Dearing CB

The Rt Hon John Patten MP
Secretary of State for Education
Department for Education
Sanctuary Buildings
Great Smith Street
London, SW1P 3BT

20 December 1993

Dear Secretary of State,

I have pleasure in enclosing my final report on the remit you gave me on 7 April to look into the scope for slimming down the National Curriculum and related issues.

As you will recall, the Interim Report in July made a number of firm proposals on slimmed down national tests in the core subjects, and indicated a broad way forward on the National Curriculum. This Report is concerned with developing that preliminary thinking on the National Curriculum into firm recommendations. It also makes recommendations to you and to the Secretary of State for Wales on the development of the quality and standing of teacher assessment; on reducing the work connected with that; and on the ten-level scale. I have been consulted by the Curriculum Council for Wales on the assessment of Welsh second language, and endorse their advice.

May I say how much I appreciated the encouragement from you to explore fully the issues opened up by the remit and to make substantive proposals to slim down the statutory curriculum. The National Curriculum has the wide support of the teaching profession, but I believe it needs the kind of changes invited by your remit.

I am much indebted to Chris Woodhead for his contribution to the Review and the preparation of this Report, and to my Authority colleagues, particularly those on the Advisory Group, for the time and wisdom they so generously offered. While the responsibility for the Report is mine, I owe much to others, and particularly to the teachers who responded so fully to the opportunity to comment on the issues you raised.

I am copying this letter and my Report to the Secretary of State for Wales.

Yours sincerely,

Ron Dearing

1   TERMS OF REFERENCE AND DEFINITIONS

Terms of reference of the Review

1.1   On 7 April 1993, the Secretary of State for Education invited me to undertake a Review of the National Curriculum and of the framework for assessing pupils' progress. The issues I was asked to cover in the Review were:

i   the scope for slimming down the curriculum;

ii   how the central administration of the National Curriculum and testing arrangements could be improved;

iii   how the testing arrangements might be simplified; and

iv   the future of the ten-level scale for recognising children's attainment.

1.2   Following extensive consultation, an Interim Report to Ministers in July 1993 made a number of recommendations on the first three issues above, which were accepted by Government. These recommendations, and Ministers' response to them, are summarised in Appendix 1. The Interim Report also identified three issues for further work and consultation:

i   the future shape of the curriculum for 14 to 16 year olds;

ii   the timetable for slimming down the curriculum: whether streamlining should be introduced in all subjects simultaneously or over a period of time;

iii   the future grading of pupils' attainments based either on retention of the existing ten-level scale, with some improvements, or on a replacement. (This further consideration of the ten-level scale and alternatives to it reflected the fact that the consultation had identified a range of problems with the scale but no clear view as to the best way forward.)

1.3   Ministers supported further consultation on these issues in their response to the Interim Report. A second phase of consultation has accordingly taken place through the autumn. It covered these three points. It also invited comment on the amount of time the National Curriculum should occupy at each key stage.

1.4 This Report offers recommendations on these issues. It also carries forward a number of other matters identified for further consideration in the Interim Report, including special educational needs; the place of moderated teacher assessment in the measurement of pupil achievement; and the potential use of a value-added approach to the evaluation of school performance.

1.5 The Report relates primarily to the National Curriculum and assessment in England. The Secretary of State for Wales invited the Curriculum Council for Wales (CCW) to undertake a Review in that country relating to the slimming down of the curriculum, the curriculum at Key Stage 4, and the assessment of Welsh second language. Recommendations on these matters in Wales are the subject of a separate report from CCW to the Secretary of State for Wales. On the ten-level scale, this Report responds to requests for advice from Ministers in England and Wales. Similarly, my further recommendations on teacher assessment in non-core subjects relate to both countries. In some cases these recommendations propose further work by the School Curriculum and Assessment Authority. It will be for the Curriculum and Assessment Authority for Wales, which assumes responsibility for National Curriculum assessment in Wales from 1 April 1994, to consider how this work should be taken forward in Wales after that date.

Definitions

1.6 All specialisms have their technical vocabularies and the National Curriculum is no exception. The main specialist terms used in this Report are defined in the following paragraphs.

1.7 The **National Curriculum**, as defined by the Education Reform Act 1988, consists of ten **foundation subjects** (eleven in Wales) which state maintained schools are required by law to teach. Some of the foundation subjects - English, mathematics, science, and, in Wales, Welsh - are designated as **core subjects**. The other foundation subjects are art, geography, history, music, physical education and technology, with a modern foreign language for pupils from the age of 11 and, in Wales, Welsh second language. After the age of 14, some options are available: students may drop art and music; they may drop either history or geography or follow a short course in each; and they may choose to follow short courses in technology and a modern foreign language. Religious education is not part of the National Curriculum, but all schools are required by law to teach it. From September 1994, sex education will also be a statutory requirement in Key Stages 3 and 4.

1.8   The National Curriculum is structured in four **key stages** or phases of learning:

- **Key Stage 1** - pupils aged 5 to 7
- **Key Stage 2** - pupils aged 7 to 11
- **Key Stage 3** - pupils aged 11 to 14
- **Key Stage 4** - students aged 14 to 16.

1.9   The curriculum for each subject is set out in statutory subject **Orders** which specify **programmes of study** (the matters, skills and processes to be taught) and **attainment targets** (the knowledge, skills and understanding to be acquired).

1.10   In all subjects other than art, music and physical education, each attainment target is arranged hierarchically in ten levels of achievement, known as the **ten-level scale**. These levels define the academic progress pupils can make between the ages of 5 and 16. Typically a pupil is expected to advance one level every two years. Only the most gifted are expected to achieve level 10 by the age of 16. Some children with severe learning difficulties may not progress beyond the first level. An average student will achieve level 6 or level 7 by the age of 16.

1.11   **Statements of attainment** seek to define what a pupil should know, understand and be able to do at each level. For art, music and physical education, **end of key stage statements** summarise what a pupil should know, understand and be able to do by the end of each key stage.

1.12   The day to day assessment of a pupil's progress to diagnose learning needs and to plan future programmes of teaching is undertaken according to policies decided by individual schools. This is sometimes known as **formative assessment**. In addition, **standard tests** (often referred to as national tests) are taken in certain subjects (currently English, Welsh, mathematics and science) at the end of the key stage. In 1994, such tests will for the first time be taken at the end of each of the first three key stages, although the Key Stage 2 tests are a voluntary national pilot. The tests, together with teachers' summaries of their assessments, provide an overall judgement on a pupil's achievements in each subject at the end of each key stage, and contribute to reports on progress to parents. This is sometimes known as **summative assessment**.

1.13   Some children have special educational needs. A small proportion of these children have **statements of special educational need**. This means that a special statutory process has been followed to identify the pupil's needs and to indicate how these needs should be met.

2

SUMMARY OF MAIN CONCLUSIONS
AND RECOMMENDATIONS

2.1   The National Curriculum is fundamental to raising educational standards. Urgent action is needed to reduce the statutorily required content of its programmes of study and to make it less prescriptive and less complex. A closely co-ordinated review of all the statutory curriculum Orders should immediately be put in hand, guided by the need to:

i   reduce the volume of material required by law to be taught;

ii   simplify and clarify the programmes of study;

iii   reduce prescription so as to give more scope for professional judgement;

iv   ensure that the Orders are written in a way which offers maximum support to the classroom teacher.

Paragraph 3.8

Slimming the curriculum at Key Stages 1, 2 and 3

2.2   The primary purpose of the review at Key Stages 1, 2 and 3 should be to slim down the National Curriculum; to make the Orders less prescriptive; and to free some 20% of teaching time for use at the discretion of the school.

Paragraphs 4.16 and 4.29

2.3   The review should, therefore, be primarily concerned with dividing the content of the present curriculum Orders between a statutory core and optional material for use at the discretion of the school. The slimming down should take place in the context of curricular objectives for each key stage with all Orders being revised together.

Paragraphs 4.3-4.4

2.4   The first priority for discretionary time must be to support work in the basics of literacy, oracy and numeracy. Beyond this, the bulk of the time released should be used for work in those National Curriculum subjects which the school chooses to explore in more depth. In addition to the National Curriculum subjects and religious education, time must also be found at Key Stage 3 for sex education as required by law and for careers education and guidance.

Paragraphs 3.26, 4.46 and 4.47

2.5 Schools should be accountable to their governing bodies for using the time released effectively. The school's decisions should be recorded and available for inspection.

Paragraph 4.48

2.6 The review should define the essential matters, skills and processes which must be taught at each key stage and should not change the basic content of the programmes of study except where there is a clear need to do so. The more radically the Orders are changed, the greater the time schools will need to plan for their introduction.

Paragraphs 3.26, 4.33 and 8.4

2.7 The opportunity should, however, be taken to reduce the present numbers of attainment targets and statements of attainment. The scope for reducing the number of attainment targets is greatest at the lower levels. The aim in reducing the number of statements of attainment should be to produce a definition of what is expected at each level which is sufficiently clear and rigorous to be of use to teachers, but which avoids the excessive detail of the current approach.

Paragraphs 4.3vii, 4.45 and 7.29

2.8 The National Curriculum Council's (NCC) recommendations for revised attainment targets and programmes of study for English and design & technology should provide the basis for the review of these subjects. Pending the introduction of a new design & technology curriculum, schools should be able to make applications under section 16 of the Education Reform Act 1988 to teach the curriculum proposed by the NCC on an experimental basis in Key Stages 1, 2 and 3.

Paragraphs 4.36-4.37

2.9 Each National Curriculum subject should continue to be taught in the first three key stages, but the review should recognise the prime importance of mastery of the basics of learning at the primary stage, including literacy, oracy, numeracy and a basic competence in the use of information technology.

Paragraphs 4.5-4.7

2.10 The revised Orders should be presented in single volumes for Key Stages 1 and 2.

Paragraph 4.35

2.11   The review should be undertaken by the School Curriculum and Assessment Authority (SCAA) whose senior officers should be assisted by advisory groups for each key stage and subject.   Their membership should include teachers and headteachers (primary and secondary).   The SCAA should work closely with the Curriculum Council for Wales in this review, particularly in subjects for which the curriculum is common to England and Wales.

Paragraphs 4.49-4.53 and Appendix 5

2.12   Final decisions on the balance of statutory provision for the subjects should be taken in the light of advice from groups set up by the School Curriculum and Assessment Authority.   To assist the groups in this task, the Report offers guidance on the time which should be assumed to be available for each subject at each key stage.   A major reduction will be required in the content of the non-core subjects at Key Stages 1 and 2.

Paragraphs 4.20-4.32

2.13   No further major changes should be made to the National Curriculum Orders for five years following the review.

Paragraph 4.54

Revising the curriculum at Key Stage 4

2.14   At Key Stage 4, schools should have greater opportunity to offer a curriculum which meets the distinctive talents and individual aspirations of their students.   The mandatory requirements should be limited to English, mathematics and single science, physical education and short courses in a modern foreign language and technology. Religious education and sex education must, in addition, be taught by law.   Careers education is also particularly important at this key stage.   These minimum requirements will allow greater scope for academic and vocational options.

Paragraphs 5.17-5.26

2.15   As an objective for the medium term, a General National Vocational Qualification (GNVQ) option should be developed for use at Key Stage 4 as part of a wider curriculum.   But its general introduction must be dependent upon the development of courses and assessments of the highest quality.   Meanwhile, the School Curriculum and Assessment Authority (SCAA) should discuss with the National Council for Vocational Qualifications (NCVQ) whether and how work undertaken as part of GCSE courses could count towards GNVQ accreditation.   The SCAA should continue, in particular, to discuss with the NCVQ the possibility of a 'Part One' qualification for the foundation and intermediate levels of the GNVQ.

Paragraphs 5.31-5.39 and 5.42-5.43

2.16   Further thought should be given to the introduction of a National Vocational Qualification option as part of a wider curriculum at Key Stage 4.

Paragraph 5.40

2.17   The present requirement for National Curriculum short courses to be combined with another short course for accreditation purposes should be abandoned. Urgent attention should be given as to how free-standing short courses might best be accredited.

Paragraph 5.44

2.18   The School Curriculum and Assessment Authority should consult the GCSE examining boards on whether the scope for offering somewhat different syllabuses in the GCSE examinations should be enlarged by reducing the content of the National Curriculum subjects which is statutorily prescribed.

Paragraph 5.47

2.19   The recommendation that history and geography should no longer be mandatory subjects in Key Stage 4 should take immediate effect to avoid uncertainty in schools, examining bodies and publishers.

Paragraph 5.49

2.20   Pending the introduction of a revised Order for technology in 1996 at Key Stage 4 (1995 for Key Stages 1, 2 and 3), this subject should not be compulsory for students entering Key Stage 4 in 1994 and 1995.

Paragraph 5.50

Accountability and Reporting

2.21   The increased trust placed in schools and teachers by reducing prescription in the curriculum and freeing up time for use at their own discretion should be complemented by proper accountability to parents and more widely through the provision of information, including that from simple, national tests in the core subjects, about progress and achievement.

Paragraphs 3.34-3.40

2.22   The School Curriculum and Assessment Authority should accept full accountability for its performance and publish an annual report to the Secretary of State for Education reporting on its work, good and bad.

Paragraphs 3.41-3.43

Special educational needs

2.23   The National Curriculum should be available to pupils with special educational needs.

Paragraph 6.4i

2.24   The National Curriculum levels defined in the Orders should be broadened to include level 1 at Key Stage 2 and levels 1 and 2 at Key Stage 3 to ensure that teachers can provide work wholly in line with their pupils' abilities and needs.

Paragraph 6.4ii

2.25   .The work on the revision of the National Curriculum should involve teachers of pupils with special educational needs.

Paragraph 6.4iii

2.26   Schools should liaise with parents over the development of the appropriate curriculum for statemented pupils.

Paragraph 6.5

2.27   The assessment and recording of the achievements of pupils with special educational needs (including the provision of non-statutory test material) should be reviewed by the School Curriculum and Assessment Authority (SCAA). As a first step, the SCAA should commission a study of previous work in this area by schools, local education authorities and other agencies with a view to providing guidance material for general use.

Paragraphs 6.8 and 9.15

The ten-level scale

2.28   The ten-level scale is unnecessarily complex and excessively prescriptive. It suffers from duplication and inconsistencies. These failings explain some very real problems teachers have experienced in implementing the National Curriculum.

Paragraphs 7.15-7.25

2.29   The purposes it was intended to serve are nevertheless sound.

Paragraph 7.24

2.30   Not all of the problems associated with the ten-level scale can be resolved, but much can be done to improve it.

Paragraphs 7.21-7.37

2.31   The alternative key stage scale, which has been the subject of consultation, avoids some of the inherent problems of the ten-level scale. It could incorporate the kind of improvements which can be made to the ten-level scale. But it too has disadvantages, and it has not as yet been tested in the classroom. There are, therefore, uncertainties involved in making a change to it, and consultation showed no consensus for change.

Paragraphs 7.38-7.46

2.32   Bearing in mind the foregoing points and the need to give first priority to revising the curriculum and securing its early implementation in schools, the ten-level scale should be retained but improved.

Paragraph 7.60

2.33   The improvements to be made are:

i   a substantial reduction in the number of statements of attainment to provide a definition of what is expected at each level, which is sufficiently clear and rigorous to be of use to teachers but which avoids the excessive detail of the present approach;

Paragraphs 7.26-7.30

ii   a reduction in the number of attainment targets to reflect the slimming down of the statutorily required curriculum (particularly at Key Stages 1 and 2);

Paragraph 7.27

iii   the definition, where necessary, of more even steps between levels.

Paragraph 7.31

2.34   The ten-level scale should finish at the end of Key Stage 3. Student achievement in Key Stage 4 should be accredited through GCSE grades and, where appropriate, other approved qualifications. The School Curriculum and Assessment Authority should give further thought to how best to accredit the achievement of students who do not reach the standard associated with GCSE Grade G.

Paragraphs 7.62-7.64

2.35 Art, music and physical education should continue to be assessed through end of key stage statements.

Paragraph 7.52

The approach to revising and introducing the curriculum

2.36 The curriculum Orders should be revised simultaneously.

Paragraph 8.1

2.37 Given the need to deal as quickly as possible with the present problems of curriculum overload and to free up time for use at the discretion of the school, the School Curriculum and Assessment Authority should manage the process of slimming down the statutory content of the curricula with a view to schools introducing the revised Orders in September 1995 for Key Stages 1, 2 and 3. The new Orders should be introduced simultaneously in all years of these key stages.

Paragraphs 8.2-8.7

2.38 Given that the core subjects will not be subject to much change and that the School Curriculum and Assessment Authority is committed to providing schools with information on national tests in good time, these tests in the core subjects should continue uninterrupted.

Paragraph 8.8

2.39 There should be urgent discussions with the GCSE examining boards about the feasibility of 1996 as the starting date for new GCSE syllabuses.

Paragraph 8.12

Teacher assessment in the non-core subjects and value-added

2.40 The School Curriculum and Assessment Authority should continue to simplify the national tests in the core subjects as far as possible without sacrificing validity and reliability. In particular, the time which is needed to administer the tests must continue to be reduced.

Paragraphs 3.31, 3.42 and 7.10

13

2.41　In support of moderated teacher assessment, the School Curriculum and Assessment Authority should be prepared to produce further material similar to that in the *Children's/Pupils' Work Assessed* series.　It should also provide test material and marking schemes, or validate such material provided by other agencies, for use at the discretion of schools to assist them in their assessment of pupils' work.

Paragraphs 9.4-9.5 and 9.15

2.42　The key aim in developing systems of moderated teacher assessment must be to develop an approach which underpins standards but which is neither bureaucratic nor excessive in its call on teacher time.

Paragraph 9.3

2.43　Until the revision of the Orders has taken place and the number of attainment targets and statements of attainment has been reduced, statutory teacher assessment should not be required beyond the core subjects in primary schools.　The issue of when statutory teacher assessment should be introduced and what form it should take should be reviewed once the new curriculum Orders have been implemented.

Paragraph 9.9

2.44　Once the decision is taken following the revision of the Orders to extend statutory teacher assessment to the non-core subjects in primary schools, then the separate decision on the introduction of statutory moderation arrangements should only be taken after a careful evaluation by the School Curriculum and Assessment Authority.

Paragraph 9.10

2.45　Further advice should be given to primary schools on how the level of record keeping, which has been a heavy burden for many teachers, can be reduced.　This advice is set out in Appendix 6, and has been agreed with the Office for Standards in Education and the Office of Her Majesty's Chief Inspector of Schools in Wales.

Paragraph 9.11 and Appendix 6

2.46　For Key Stage 3, statutory teacher assessment of non-core subjects should be introduced or reintroduced when the revision of the curriculum Orders has taken place and schools have had time to adapt to them.　But no decision should be taken on the moderation of statutory teacher assessment pending the outcome of present consultation with teachers on its purposes and form.

Paragraphs 9.13-9.14

2.47　The Group set up by the School Curriculum and Assessment Authority to advise on the value-added approach to the measurement of school performance should report by June 1994.

Paragraphs 9.16-9.17

3

INTRODUCTION

"Upon the education of the people of this country, the future of this country depends."

3.1 If this was true when Disraeli spoke these words in 1874 when Britain was at the height of its economic power, it is even more so today. In a highly competitive world there is nowhere to hide. The fact that standards of educational achievement are rising internationally, and, in particular, in the Far East, means that our future as a nation depends upon the improvements we can make to our education system.

3.2 The evidence is that, while academically gifted students fully match international standards, those who are of average ability or whose talents are not academic are faring less well. In the long term, this failure to realise the potential of all our young people will undermine our economic performance and quality of life. This is a matter for profound concern.

3.3 The central aim of this Review must be to make proposals which will both support and challenge teachers in their task. It is teachers and only teachers who can directly improve educational standards. I have, therefore, sought to involve teachers to the greatest possible extent in the work leading to this Report.

The approach to the second stage of the Review

3.4 The second stage of the Review, like the first, has accordingly involved wide consultation. With the assistance of teachers, papers were prepared which were discussed at eight consultation meetings in England, each of which was attended by 50 or more teachers and headteachers. Similar meetings were held in Wales by the Curriculum Council for Wales. Other meetings have been held with specialist groups, notably on matters relating to children with special educational needs and on the ten-level scale.

3.5 In addition, with the help of the *Times Educational Supplement* which printed articles setting out the issues and inviting readers to write to me with their views, some 1,400 written reports have been received from teachers, schools and other interested parties. Contributions have also been received from industry and commerce; from specialist associations; from parent and governor associations; from local education authorities;

from the Office for Standards in Education; from teachers' professional associations; and from experts in various aspects of education.

The principles guiding this Review

3.6 This Review was instituted by the Secretary of State for Education in response to widespread concern that the basic aims of the National Curriculum and its assessment arrangements were being undermined by complexity, over-elaboration, over-prescription and excessive content.

3.7 Teachers have reiterated these concerns throughout the Review. Their commitment to the principle of the National Curriculum is clear, but so, too, is the need for urgent and immediate action to ensure that the curriculum is rendered manageable and that the burden of administration is reduced.

3.8 The consultation leads me to believe that we can help teachers do a better job for their pupils with the National Curriculum by:

   i   reducing the volume of material required by law to be taught;

   ii   simplifying and clarifying the programmes of study;

   iii   reducing prescription so as to give more scope for professional judgement;

   iv   ensuring that the Orders are written in a way which offers maximum support to the classroom teacher.

3.9 Given the expectation for change which my terms of reference and the associated consultation have created over the last eight months, there may be some who feel I should have been more radical. But there is much good in what has been achieved so far. We can build upon the enormous commitment in time and energy which teachers have made to the National Curriculum. There is no sense whatsoever in seeking to start all over again. There is wisdom in the warning that to seek constantly after perhaps illusory improvement is to use time and energy which would be better devoted to making the present arrangements work.

3.10   We should not take risks with the education of millions of pupils. My personal accountability to these pupils means that I must be confident that the case for any change is well-founded.

The Educational Challenge

3.11   Education is not concerned only with equipping students with the knowledge and skills they need to earn a living. It must help our young people to: use leisure time creatively; have respect for other people, other cultures and other beliefs; become good citizens; think things out for themselves; pursue a healthy life-style; and, not least, value themselves and their achievements. It should develop an appreciation of the richness of our cultural heritage and of the spiritual and moral dimensions to life. It must, moreover be concerned to serve all our children well, whatever their background, sex, creed, ethnicity or talent.

3.12   It is the primary school teacher who must begin to fulfil these objectives. I am very conscious of the challenge many primary school teachers face, receiving as they do children from very different backgrounds - social, economic, ethnic, religious - and varying greatly in their readiness to learn. But if children do not leave primary school with a firm grasp of the basic skills of literacy and numeracy, with an appetite for learning and with a belief in themselves and their talents, their future progress will inevitably be stunted.

3.13   In the primary school, the teacher is greatly helped by the natural enthusiasm, openness and curiosity of young children. Secondary school pupils may well, however, have lost some of this innate enthusiasm and motivation becomes an issue. As they grow older, they are likely to develop their own particular interests and aspirations. We need to recognise their emerging abilities and aspirations if we are to motivate each and every one of our pupils to achieve their potential.

3.14   The Government has responded to the challenge of matching standards in this country with the best in the world by supporting national targets for education and training which have been established by leaders in the world of work. The targets (usually expressed in terms of National Vocational Qualifications but represented for the purposes of this report in GCSE and A level terms) most immediately relevant to schools are:

- By 1997, 80% of young people to gain four GCSEs at Grades A-C or the vocational equivalent.

- By 2000, 50% of young people to gain two GCE A-level passes or the vocational equivalent.

3.15   The levels of achievement underlying these targets will be realised only if we can ensure that all pupils master the knowledge, understanding and skills required by the National Curriculum Orders for the core subjects and develop a basic competence in the use of information technology. These are the foundations of progress in education and training, and a continuing theme in this Report.

3.16   The achievement of the national targets depends no less on acceptance of our national responsibility to develop the talents of all our young people. To have 80% gain the equivalent of four GCSEs at grades A to C or their vocational equivalent by 1997 requires a major improvement in the achievement of a large number of students, including those not at present responding well to formal academic approaches to education. In 1992, for example, only 47% of students gained four GCSEs at Grades A-C. To achieve the national targets, we need to recognise that it may be more effective for some students to pursue educational goals in a vocational context, and, more fundamentally, to broaden our concept of achievement.

3.17   This need to respond to the many-sidedness of talent underlies the development of three broad educational pathways in post-16 education and training:

- the 'craft' or 'occupational' - equipping young people with particular skills and with knowledge directly related to a craft or occupation through National Vocational Qualifications (NVQs).

- the 'vocational' - a midway path between the academic and occupational - leading to General National Vocational Qualifications (GNVQs).

- the 'academic', leading to A and AS levels.

3.18   The development of the three pathways for post-16 education raises the question of whether, and if so to what extent, students aged 14 to 16 should be able to follow a well-devised vocational course as one element in a broadly based curriculum. A decision on this issue needs to be taken in the context, on the one hand, of avoiding a student making a premature commitment to one pathway and thereby cutting off important options for the future, and, on the other, of the need to respond to the distinctive talents of students and to provide motivation to learn across the whole spectrum of aptitudes so that the nation can achieve its targets for education and training. In short, with full-time education and training post-16 becoming the norm, we should see the age of 14 as the beginning of an educational continuum from 14 to 19, but one which does not commit the student prematurely to a narrow track.

3.19   The Government is right to state that the alternative pathways must be of equal quality, leading to parity of esteem. Our historic commitment as a nation to a liberal humanist concept of education was well expressed in John Stuart Mill's Rectorial address to the University of St.Andrews in 1867, when he said:

> *"Men are men before they are lawyers, or physicians, or merchants,*
> *or manufacturers; and if you make them capable and sensible men,*
> *they will make themselves capable and sensible lawyers or physicians".*

3.20   That is a telling comment. We need, nevertheless, to consider whether a vocational and/or occupational element in a more broadly based education post-14 is an option which will serve better to develop some young people into capable and sensible men and women than an education that does not offer that possibility. There is little support for a narrowly based vocational education before 16, but the view of many teachers and others is that it would be right to include such an option as part of a broadly based curriculum. It would not, however, be desirable to make a major commitment to vocational qualifications in Key Stage 4 while these qualifications are still at a developmental stage.

3.21   Meanwhile, it is right that some schools should be collaborating in the development of this route. There are already options available to students who wish to follow courses based upon the application of knowledge offered through the GCSE and qualifications of the Business and Technology Education Council, the City and Guilds of London Institute and the Royal Society of Arts Examinations Board.

Scope for professional judgement

3.22   The question of how much time the National Curriculum should occupy is central to the second stage of my Review.

3.23 Teachers believe that the National Curriculum has brought a new and valuable breadth to pupils' learning. The argument has been put repeatedly at consultation meetings that children are entitled to a broadly based education and should be safeguarded against the narrow curriculum which some have experienced in the past. Her Majesty's Inspectors report that the combined effect of the National Curriculum and national assessment has challenged teachers' assumptions of what their pupils can achieve and has, as a consequence, helped to raise standards. Such reports justify the broad strategy of the present approach.

3.24 The National Curriculum was never, however, intended to occupy the whole of school time. The prevailing view when the Education Reform Bill was before Parliament was that it should occupy some 70-80%, leaving the balance for use at the discretion of the school. A margin for use at the discretion of the school is needed in the interests of providing the best possible education. It provides scope for the school to draw upon particular strengths in its teaching staff; to take advantage of learning opportunities provided by the local environment; and to respond to the needs and enthusiasms of particular children.

3.25 By contrast it is clear from the consultation that has informed each stage of the Review that most teachers think that the National Curriculum as presently laid down cannot be taught in the minimum weekly teaching time recommended by the Department for Education (DFE). They strongly support a slimming down of the curriculum and, typically, counsel that around 20% of time at Key Stages 1 to 3 should be for use at the discretion of the school. While Her Majesty's Chief Inspector of Schools has drawn attention to wide differences in the length of the teaching week between schools, and there is a substantial number where the time for teaching does not match the minimum recommended by the DFE, I am satisfied that there is a general problem of excess content in the curriculum affecting the school community as a whole.

3.26 The provision of such a margin of time beyond the reduced statutory National Curriculum and religious education has to be reconciled with teachers' strong professional commitment to the teaching of basic skills of literacy, oracy and numeracy in the early years and to the provision of a properly broad and balanced curriculum. This reconciliation has often proved to be a particularly demanding challenge in the consultation process. But I believe that it can be achieved through a division of the content of the present National Curriculum Orders into the essential matters, skills and processes which every school must by law teach and the optional material which can be taught according to the professional judgement of teachers. I also believe that, while teachers may choose not to use the optional material, they can and, indeed, should, use the bulk of the time released to develop pupils' education within the broad areas covered by the National Curriculum. Time will also be required for sex education in Key Stages 3 and 4, and for careers education.

3.27   There is, of course, a risk that poor schools might use the discretionary time unwisely. It must not be forgotten that the National Curriculum was introduced to raise standards and expectations and to ensure that all children had access to the same educational entitlement. Standards of educational achievement will fall unless headteachers and governing bodies ensure that time released is used to give children the best possible education. Schools will need to show their governing bodies and parents that they are using the time effectively.

Using the teacher's time more effectively

3.28   One of my concerns throughout this Review has been to help to ensure that teachers' time, by far the most valuable resource a school possesses, is used to maximum effect. This concern underpinned the recommendations made in the Interim Report that:

i   there should be stability in the curriculum for two years;

ii   the statutory tests should be halved for most pupils and confined to the core subjects for the next three years;

iii   the scale of recording pupils' progress against each statement of attainment should be greatly reduced.

3.29   Since the publication of the Interim Report, in association with Her Majesty's Chief Inspectors of Schools in England and Wales, I have given further advice on how the burden of recording can be reduced. The Government has also decided to postpone the introduction of the National Curriculum Orders at Key Stage 4 for history and geography pending decisions on the recommendations in this Report. The recommendations made in the Interim Report on deferring the extended adoption of statutory teacher assessment eased the detailed work involved in assessment and reporting to parents.

3.30   This Report makes further contributions to the more effective use of teachers' time by its proposals to:

i   reduce the amount of material in each Order which has statutorily to be taught;

ii   reduce greatly the number of statements of attainment and cut the number of attainment targets, thus further reducing the scale of recording, marking and reporting which teachers undertake;

iii   render the Orders easier to use by setting out their content in a more accessible and helpful way and by providing the entire content of the National Curriculum in single documents for Key Stages 1 and 2.

3.31   In addition, the Report offers help to teachers through its recommendations on statutory teacher assessment and advice to teachers on recording pupils' progress in primary schools. It recommends urgent action by the School Curriculum and Assessment Authority to find ways to cut down the administrative work connected with national tests. In that general context, I attach particular weight to the remit of the Office for Standards in Education to comment on the efficient use of resources, including teachers' time, in relation to the basic objective of raising educational achievement.

3.32   It is no part of my thinking that the proposed reduction in the content of the statutory curriculum should result - for pupils or teachers - in a less rigorous and less demanding curriculum. Were this to happen, the Review would have served education badly. My concern is, rather, to release more of teachers' energies for teaching. But I believe the reductions proposed will lift the burden of anxiety felt by many teachers, particularly in primary schools, because of their inability to teach the whole of an over-provided curriculum. Moreover, I believe that the trust this places in teachers will serve to encourage the profession in its vital task of raising educational standards.

The contribution of parents

3.33   All involved in education recognise the great benefit to a child's progress that comes from the active support and involvement of parents. This is particularly so in the early years. Not all parents are themselves well-equipped to offer assistance, but, by showing strong interest in their child's achievements, by encouraging reading, by taking advantage of everyday occurrences to widen the child's understanding and knowledge, all parents can help greatly. This matter lies beyond the remit of this Review, but, if ways could be found to involve more mothers and fathers in the initial teaching of reading, we would make a huge contribution to the raising of educational standards. Parents must accept that the responsibility for the education of young children is one they share with the school: they handicap their child for life if they do not give the school the support the child needs to give of his or her best.

Schools' accountability to parents and society

3.34   Schools have a fundamental responsibility for the future well-being of our nation. They must, therefore, be accountable to parents and society as a whole. I believe teachers accept this. The issue is the form that this accountability should take.

3.35   Parents have a right to be informed about both the progress of their child and the performance of the school as a whole in the light of the continuing assessments being made by teachers and simple national tests in the core subjects at the end of the first three key stages. Parental support for the child's learning and support for the school and its teachers is more likely to be offered if a policy of openness is pursued. If a school has difficulties with behaviour, truancy or disappointing academic results, these problems, alongside its strengths and achievements, should be shared with its parents.

3.36   Parents who are choosing a school for their child should have access to a wide range of information about the school's ethos, curriculum and performance.

3.37   More generally, the nation has a need to know, at local and national level, how its schools are performing. Truancy and poor performance spell trouble for the future. Children who want to go to school and who are developing their talents are potentially good citizens. Only with information can the local community - parents, employers, local authorities, the churches and other faith communities, and interested associations - support schools in their work. At national level, information about the achievement of our children and the performance of schools is critical to the future well-being of the whole country.

3.38   On-going teacher assessment is central to the assessment of the performance of the individual child. This Report describes the action taken since the Interim Report to identify ways to help teachers improve the quality and enhance the standing of their assessment, and makes further proposals to this end. Teacher assessment needs to be complemented with information from short, well-conceived national tests in the core subjects at the end of each key stage. Such tests occur only three times in a child's school days.

3.39 It is relevant to refer here to a very recent report from the Office for Standards in Education which states that:

> "The assessment requirements of the National Curriculum have a vital role in raising the expectations of teachers, pupils and parents. In particular, assessment should ensure that individual learning is more clearly targeted and that shortcomings are quickly identified and remedied, thus contributing towards higher standards overall. Despite the difficulties encountered during this year, National Curriculum assessment has produced clear benefits in working towards these objectives. Teacher assessment and statutory testing have both played a part in improving teachers' understanding of the National Curriculum and of the standards that are expected; taken together they have done much to ensure that the whole of the National Curriculum is taught and assessed. As a result, teachers are setting more demanding targets for learning across a broader range of curricular experiences."

3.40 This Report argues that more must be left to the professional judgement of teachers. The statutory content of the programmes of study is to be slimmed, the number of attainment targets and statements of attainment reduced, and the need for detailed record keeping cut back. This increased trust in teachers, which I believe is very much in the interests of education, should, however, be matched by accountability to parents and society, including that from simple tests in the core subjects.

The accountability of the School Curriculum and Assessment Authority

3.41 I have referred to the responsibilities of parents and schools. The School Curriculum and Assessment Authority, too, has great responsibilities: for advising the Government on the National Curriculum and on statutory assessment; and for the quality of public examinations up to GCE A level.

3.42 The success of our schools depends upon the School Curriculum and Assessment Authority's ability to respond to the need for reform. The challenge we face is to slim down the statutorily required content of the curriculum in a way that is responsive to the needs of the child and its parents, the school and society as a whole. It is equally important that the Authority succeeds in the task of continuing, first, to simplify national tests in the core subjects so that they provide valid information in a way that avoids excessive demands on teacher time, and, second, to help raise the quality and status of teacher assessment.

3.43 In advocating accountability to others, the Authority must accept its own accountability. I propose, therefore, that the Authority should present to the Government and publish an annual report which is as frank about its own performance as this Report suggests schools should be in their relationship with parents and with society.

Timescale for action in the Report

3.44 The Report makes recommendations on slimming down the statutory content of the National Curriculum, on the arrangements for introducing the new curricula and on the future of the ten-level scale, for implementation in September 1995 in Key Stages 1, 2 and 3 and the following year for Key Stage 4. This is a demanding timescale and I am conscious that the teaching profession wants the job done quickly, but done well. We must make all the speed we can to relieve teachers of the overload of content and an excess of prescription that is standing in the way of getting the best out of the National Curriculum. Overall, I have looked for an approach to change that builds on experience rather than one that breaks new ground.

3.45 On some major issues, the Report envisages a timescale for progressive implementation which may well extend over several years. Such initiatives include the development of: teacher moderation; of measures of value-added; and of new approaches to education between the ages of 14 and 19 which include the extension of vocational options. That is not to say that action on these important issues should be deferred: but rather that implementation will need to be undertaken progressively when we are confident that these changes will genuinely help to raise standards. As the later sections of this Report make clear, action is in hand.

Conclusion

3.46   The challenge facing the world of business and industry is as obvious as it is severe. To survive, let alone prosper, it is necessary, day in and day out, to aim for and achieve standards previously thought unobtainable. So, too, in education. The fact that the competition is not as obvious in education as in business merely makes the challenge to improve performance and raise standards the more demanding.

3.47   As a nation we are, therefore, fortunate that our teachers are deeply committed to the well-being of their pupils. I believe that a policy which trusts more to teachers' professional judgement and which cuts back on administration to free time for teaching will, coupled with an acceptance that schools are accountable to parents and society for their stewardship, produce the results we need.

4.1   The task is to devise a curriculum for each key stage which will help teachers to raise educational standards; which recognises the distinct learning needs of pupils as they progress through the key stages; which provides for children of widely differing talents and aptitudes; which is manageable in terms of volume but no less challenging than the existing curriculum; and which recognises that there must be room for schools to exercise professional judgement on how best to respond to the particular needs of their pupils.

4.2   This Section deals with Key Stages 1, 2 and 3 together because all nine (ten in Key Stage 3) National Curriculum subjects should continue to be taught in these key stages. The central question here is one of how the statutory Orders should be slimmed down. In Key Stage 4, the issue is, rather, which subjects should continue to be part of the statutory requirement. Key Stage 4 is, therefore, discussed separately in Section 5 of this Report.

Summary of views expressed during consultation

4.3   The views expressed in consultation on the approach to revising the curricula may be summarised as follows.

i   The content of the National Curriculum is excessive and should be slimmed down.

ii   The slimming down of the curricula must be undertaken in the context of curricular objectives for each key stage so as to ensure that the needs of pupils at various stages in their development are met appropriately, and that the Orders collectively are both manageable and coherent.

iii   The National Curriculum Orders must, therefore, be revised together rather than sequentially.

iv   The overall approach should be to divide the existing programmes of study of the National Curriculum Orders into statutory elements which must be taught by all schools and non-statutory material which will be available for schools to use in the light of their particular circumstances and professional judgement of what best meets the needs of their pupils.

v   The degree of prescription should be reduced, although many primary teachers who have to teach the whole curriculum have said that a detailed exposition of what is required can be of practical assistance.

vi   The work on slimming down the statutory content of the present programmes of study must be informed by clear guidance on the time that should be assumed for each subject at each key stage, but it must be left to the individual school to decide precisely how much time is needed to teach each subject.

vii   The slimming down of content should be associated with a review of the number of attainment targets and a reduction in the statements of attainment.

viii   While the task of slimming down the curriculum should be completed as quickly as possible, the review must be undertaken thoroughly and rigorously, and must draw upon the views and experience of practising teachers from all key stages.

4.4   I accept all these points, and recommend that they should guide the work on slimming down the curriculum that lies ahead.

4.5   The views expressed in consultation on the key curricular objectives which should be pursued were as follows.

i   All the present subjects of the National Curriculum should continue to be studied at Key Stages 1, 2 and 3 because they provide a broad and balanced entitlement for all pupils.

ii   The prime responsibility of teachers at Key Stage 1, and to a very considerable degree at Key Stage 2, must, nevertheless, be to ensure that all pupils make good progress in the basic skills of oracy, literacy and numeracy.

iii   A proportion of school time should be made available for use at the discretion of the school. The school should be accountable for using that time well.

4.6   There was also support for the view expressed in the Interim Report that the basics of information technology should be regarded as a core skill.

4.7   Again, I believe these comments are well-founded and I recommend that they should be taken up in the work that lies ahead.

4.8   On the amount of time that should be released for use at the discretion of the school, the Interim Report made a tentative proposal that the percentage of time available for use at local discretion should progressively increase from 10-15% at Key Stage 1 to between 20-25% at Key Stage 3. The weight of opinion in consultation was that the figure should be of the order of 20% at all key stages. This central issue is discussed in detail in paragraphs 4.9-4.32 below.

Defining the time to be released for use at the discretion of schools and teachers

4.9   The Interim Report discussed releasing time for teachers in terms of a percentage slimming down of the existing curriculum Orders. It is clear from the consultation during the autumn that, in the opinion of many teachers, the combined weight of the National Curriculum is, for the typical teacher teaching a typical class, in excess of the teaching time available. A reliable quantification of the excess is not possible. Some teachers put it at 20%, but the figure depends on the teacher, the class, and the degree of depth to which the subjects are taught.

4.10   This uncertainty about the precise weight of the National Curriculum means that, instead of achieving a reduction in the mandatory National Curriculum by making percentage reductions in the content of each subject, it will be advisable instead to proceed by considering the time that should be taken as available for the statutorily prescribed element in each programme of study. This is not, I must stress, to prescribe how schools should allocate their time, but to guide the work on slimming down the statutory content of the Orders.

4.11   Her Majesty's Chief Inspector of Schools has recently drawn attention to an unacceptably wide variation of the teaching time in a school day or week. The variation can be as much as almost one full day a week. The time allocations for each subject in each key stage set out in paragraphs 4.20 and 4.31 below are expressed as hours per year, based on the Department for Education's recommended minimum weekly teaching hours (21 hours per week for Key Stage 1, 23½ for Key Stage 2 and 24 for Key Stage 3). I assume a 36 week teaching year to allow a margin for the induction of new pupils, assessment work, school events and educational visits. It is, however, very clear that those schools which are currently teaching less than the minimum weekly hours need to look hard at whether they should increase their teaching time so as to achieve better curriculum coverage.

Key Stages 1 and 2

4.12   The distinctive purpose of Key Stage 1, which covers two years, is to lay the foundation of future learning by:

i   developing the basic skills in reading, writing, speaking, listening, number and information technology;

ii   introducing young children to a broad range of interesting content spanning the subjects of the curriculum;

iii   promoting positive attitudes to learning and helping young children to work and play together harmoniously.

4.13   Key Stage 2 covers four years. Over such a long period the learning needs of children will gradually change. As they become more proficient in their reading and writing, the time they need for English will gradually reduce and, as a consequence, more time will be available for science and the foundation subjects.

4.14   The work on slimming down the statutory content of the programmes of study must be sensitive to the changing needs of children in this period. The transition throughout the four years is too gradual to lend itself to clear cut definitions of the distinctive needs at various stages, but as an illustration of the change, the distinctive purposes of the first two years might be described as:

i   the development and consolidation of the basic skills of oracy, literacy, numeracy and information technology through a range of subject content;

ii   the development of the knowledge, skills and understanding defined in the individual National Curriculum Orders.

4.15   In the second two years they are:

i   the consolidation of basic skills and the development of higher order skills;

ii   the extension of subject specific knowledge, understanding and skills.

4.16   I am satisfied that there are important gains to be had for education by giving real scope for the exercise of teacher discretion as Parliament intended, and that a provision of 20% of teaching time for this would be well-judged. The achievement of such a margin does, however, mean some hard decisions about what should remain as a statutory requirement in the programmes of study.

4.17   The discussion in the consultation conferences confirmed the paramount need to provide adequate time for the teaching of basic oracy, literacy and numeracy. As teachers argue strongly, the future success of children's education depends upon their becoming literate and numerate. English typically takes at least 30% of time at Key Stage 1 (some 25% at Key Stage 2). In addition, significant time must be found for mathematics, and, to a lesser but still important extent, for science, information technology and religious education. Given these inescapable realities, the only way of freeing up 20% of time for use at the school's discretion (when the starting point is a curriculum that exceeds 100% of the time available) is some sizeable reductions in the statutorily required provision for the other foundation subjects. Indeed, in the consultation conferences, on occasion it seemed an almost impossible task to release this amount of time in primary schools.

4.18   The problem is, however, less daunting than the arithmetic at times suggested, in that the teaching of science, geography, history and other foundation subjects provides rich opportunities for the teaching of basic literacy and, to a lesser extent, numeracy. Specific time will, of course, have to be set aside for work on English, but, in that all National Curriculum subjects involve language skills, the full 30% of teaching time which English requires at Key Stage 1 and 25% at Key Stage 2 does not have to be found in addition to the time given to other subjects.

4.19   Indeed, it is a particular feature of learning in the early years that much of it is mutually re-enforcing. For example, in history and geography a child's skills in writing and drawing may be practised; technology and science are closely related and often overlap; religious education involves historical knowledge and so on. This means that it is possible to free up something approaching 20% of time in Key Stages 1 and 2, even though the nominal sum of the content of the individual Orders in the early years would add up to the arithmetical equivalent of 90% of time. This is not sleight of hand: it is a statement of fact based on the realities of teaching at Key Stages 1 and 2 as expressed by teachers.

4.20   Taking all these considerations into account, I recommend that some 20% of teaching time can and should be freed for use at the discretion of schools and teachers at Key Stages 1 and 2 by slimming down the statutory content of the curricula in these key stages on the lines set out in the table below. It will, of course, be for schools to determine exactly how much time they should allocate to particular subjects in the light of their pupils' specific needs and local teaching opportunities.

| | | **Hours per year** | |
		Key Stage 1	**Key Stage 2**
English • directly		180	162
• through other subjects		(36)	(18)
Mathematics		126	126
Science		54	72
Information technology (through other subjects)		(27)	(36)
Each of the six foundation subjects		36	45
Religious education		36	45

4.21   These recommendations assume that the knowledge, understanding and skills of information technology should be identified within the Technology Order and taught through all relevant curriculum subjects at both key stages. The time is not additional to the time suggested for individual subjects.

4.22   I refer in paragraph 4.36 below to the National Curriculum Council's (NCC) recommendations for revised curricula for English and for design & technology. Given that some language work will take place in other subjects, the NCC recommendations for English are judged to require the provision of time set out in the table above.

4.23   The NCC's recommendations for a revised design & technology curriculum reduce the present content by about a third. This goes a long way towards the kind of slimming down needed.

4.24   While progress in the basic skills of 'number' must be strengthened at Key Stage 1, a little time will have to be found from the statutorily required content of the Mathematics Order. The Science Order will, similarly, have to be slimmed down. But these will be small reductions. Among the non-core foundation subjects, however, it is likely to mean a reduction of around half at Key Stage 1, with a similar degree of pruning at Key Stage 2.

4.25   I am conscious that the time allocation proposed for the foundation subjects does not reflect the view expressed by many teachers that music, art and physical education should occupy more time than history, geography or technology in Key Stage 1 in particular. Such fine tuning seems to be unnecessary given the release of 20% of teaching time for use at the school's discretion. Moreover, the slimming down involved in these proposals for history, geography and technology is severe, and there needs to be adequate time to provide a basic knowledge and understanding in these subjects. Final decisions on the precise balance should be taken as the detailed work begins on the revision of the Orders.

4.26   The review must recognise that practical work in science and technology and some other subjects is very time-consuming.

Key Stage 3

4.27   The curriculum in Key Stage 3 must ensure that pupils have access to a broad range of subject knowledge, understanding and skills but allow for the flexibility of approach which is needed if teachers are to motivate their pupils in different ways. Principles of breadth, access and entitlement are particularly important in this key stage if pupils are to make informed choices at Key Stage 4. A deepening understanding of the different disciplines should be seen as a natural progression from Key Stage 2. At the same time, we need to recognise that pupils are becoming more independent and clearer about their own interests. Hence the need to balance the broad entitlement with some flexibility.

4.28   In the consultation since the publication of the Interim Report, some teachers have questioned whether the depth and breadth of study required by the National Curriculum (which at this stage is enlarged to include a modern foreign language), religious education and sex education can be achieved in less than 80% of the available teaching time. The need to reach the standard required by public examinations in a modern foreign language represents a substantial additional requirement.

4.29   This was not, however, the general view, and I think it right to recommend the release of 20% of time so that there is more scope for individual schools to decide how best to motivate pupils in these key years before the run up to public examinations.

4.30 Specific provision will need to be made for information technology in Key Stage 3 so as to ensure that basic skills continue to be developed. To avoid the need for a new statutory Order, information technology should continue to be part of the Technology Order, but a distinct part of it. Specific provision for information technology is included in the table below. It will be for the school to decide how and the extent to which skills in information technology are developed through work in the different National Curriculum subjects.

4.31 The times recommended to guide the work on slimming down the National Curriculum subjects are:

	Hours per year Key Stage 3
Each of English, mathematics and science	90
Modern foreign language	63
Each of the remaining foundation subjects including information technology	45
Religious education	45

4.32 It must once again be stressed that these are figures provided to guide the work on slimming down the Orders. They are not to be seen as guidance to schools. As in Key Stages 1 and 2, final decisions on the time for each subject should be taken as the detailed work on slimming down proceeds.

The content of the National Curriculum Orders

4.33 The task ahead is to identify a slimmed down statutory content for each subject, leaving the remainder of material in the present curriculum Orders for use at the discretion of the school. It will not involve the introduction of new material. Neither will significant changes be made to the structuring of material unless there is a clear need to do so. The division between what is statutory and non-statutory, the reduction in the number of statements of attainment (see Section 7) and the reduction in the number of attainment targets proposed in paragraphs 4.43-4.45 below may well, however, result in some change in the appearance of some of the Orders.

4.34 It will be for the advisory groups (see paragraphs 4.50-4.51 below) to recommend how the School Curriculum and Assessment Authority should make the reduction of statutory content. It may be that this reduction is best achieved through the simple designation of some of the present material as discretionary, but in some instances,

35

it may be a matter of reducing prescription through providing an element of choice within the prescribed content.

4.35   It will be of great practical assistance to Key Stage 1 and 2 teachers if, following the revision of the National Curriculum Orders, the individual Orders are collected into one document for each of these key stages, and I recommend that this should be done.

4.36   The basis for the work on English and design & technology should be the programmes of study and attainment targets recommended to the Secretary of State in September 1993 by the National Curriculum Council (NCC). The proposals for design & technology already represent a slimming down of some 30% of the existing Order. It is unlikely that significant change will be needed to the English curriculum, although the NCC recommendations should be reviewed in the light of the overall recommendations of this Review.

4.37   Pending the introduction of a new Order for technology, I recommend that schools should be able to make application under section 16 of the Education Reform Act 1988 to teach the NCC's recommended curriculum on an experimental basis in Key Stages 1, 2 and 3.

4.38   An independent review of the Science Order undertaken for the NCC by Liverpool University and published in October 1993 contained proposals for major revisions to the Order.   Other authorities have also argued that this Order needs revising. Criticisms relate principally to the single science course in Key Stage 4 (see paragraph 5.48) and to Science Attainment Target 1 (Scientific Investigation), in particular at the higher levels. I recommend a substantial revision of this attainment target, but that other changes at Key Stages 1 to 3 should mainly be limited to reducing the statutorily prescribed content of the Science Order.

4.39   The structure and content of the Geography Order have been widely criticised. The proposals made above will lead to a radical reduction in statutory content and the proposals in paragraphs 4.43-4.45 below will lead to a reduction in the number of attainment targets at the lower levels. In making these reductions, the opportunity should be taken to address criticisms which have been made of the structure of the Order.

4.40 The History Order has also been subject to some criticism. The radical slimming down of the mandatory curriculum should ensure that the Order concentrates on the key knowledge, understanding and skills children should be taught in the different key stages.

4.41 Religious education is every bit as important as the subjects of the National Curriculum in that it should make a central contribution to the development of spiritual and moral understanding. The School Curriculum and Assessment Authority is currently working with the faith groups and teachers to develop model syllabuses for religious education. This work will take account of the recommendation of the time to be made available at each key stage.

4.42 Schools must also as a matter of law provide for sex education at Key Stage 3.

Reducing the number of attainment targets

4.43 Each of the National Curriculum Orders, other than that for physical education, is divided into attainment targets. These attainment targets serve to identify distinct elements within the different subjects so as to assist teachers in planning, teaching, assessing and reporting pupils' work.

4.44 The proposed revised Order for English reduces the number of attainment targets from five to three. In technology the proposed reduction is from four to two (excluding information technology).

4.45 The slimming down of the statutory content of the Orders must prompt consideration of a similar slimming down of the number of attainment targets in other Orders. To structure a National Curriculum Order, such as that for geography, which may be taught for only 36 hours a year at Key Stage 1, into five attainment targets, is to stretch credibility. I recommend that the number of attainment targets for Key Stages 1 and 2 should be subject to review. At the secondary level, it is likely that less change will be needed, but the present structure of attainment targets should be considered by the advisory groups to see whether any reduction would be appropriate, bearing in mind the reduction in the scope of the mandatory programmes of study.

The use of time released and accountability for it

4.46   In Key Stages 1 and 2, the bulk of the time released should be used for additional work in the National Curriculum subjects. The first priority must be to ensure that the basics of literacy, oracy and numeracy are adequately covered. But teachers will now have the opportunity to pursue aspects of National Curriculum subjects in greater depth according to their particular expertise and enthusiasm and the opportunities provided by the school's immediate environment. It will be for the school to decide what to teach within these broad categories. My recommendation that the bulk of the time released during Key Stages 1 and 2 be used for extension work in the subject areas of the National Curriculum should not preclude the introduction of, say, a foreign language in Key Stage 2 if the school has the expertise to do this. Many primary schools will want in the first year of Key Stage 1 to use time to help children to work in a classroom environment and to teach them how to learn.

4.47   At Key Stage 3, schools will clearly need to devote the bulk of the 20% optional time to the ten National Curriculum subjects if standards in GCSE and other public examinations are to be sustained. They must, of course, provide religious education and sex education as required by law, and careers education and guidance, but they should also be able to offer non-National Curriculum subjects such as, for example, a second modern foreign language or classics if they choose.

4.48   Schools will be accountable to their Governing Bodies for the use of the time released when the Orders are slimmed down. The school's decisions on the use of this time should be recorded and available for inspection. Parents should be told through the school's prospectus of the main decisions the school has taken.

Taking the Review forward: advisory groups

4.49   The work on revising the curricula will need to be co-ordinated carefully if it is to be carried through quickly and efficiently. The School Curriculum and Assessment Authority (SCAA) has undertaken some preliminary work, including informal consultations with a range of organisations, during the autumn. I recommend that the responsibility for the task should be given to the SCAA as the body constituted to advise on the curriculum. The SCAA should work closely with the Curriculum Council for Wales in this review, particularly in subjects for which the curriculum is common to England and Wales.

4.50   The work on slimming down the statutory content of the programmes of study must, however, include teachers and headteachers so that the new curricula can be grounded in the realities of the classroom and school planning and management. A group under the chairmanship of one of the School Curriculum and Assessment Authority's (SCAA) senior officers should, therefore, be established for each National Curriculum subject to advise on this detailed work.

4.51   The key to this whole operation will be co-ordination of these subject advisory groups at each key stage. Key stage groups constituted on the same lines as the subject groups will therefore be established to advise on the educational coherence and manageability of the Orders in the light of the distinctive needs of pupils at each key stage. A committee of SCAA members should be appointed to oversee the whole task.

4.52   The SCAA will meet the costs of cover for the teachers and headteachers involved.

4.53   Section 8 of the Report discusses the approach to implementing the new curricula in schools, and Appendix 5 outlines the timetable for the review, the role and composition of the advisory groups, and arrangements for liaison with the review in Wales.

Rolling review of National Curriculum Orders

4.54   My final recommendation in this Section is that, following this review of the National Curriculum Orders, there should be a period lasting five years in which no further major changes are made to the curriculum. This clearly makes it all the more important that the review process results in Orders which are rigorous in their educational demands but manageable in classrooms. Following this period, each Order should be reviewed according to a timetable which is published in advance.

REVISING THE CURRICULUM AT KEY STAGE 4

Introduction

5.1   The first stage of consultation revealed general support for the way in which the National Curriculum is organised in Key Stages 1, 2 and 3.   But many respondents argued that, despite action already taken by the Government to allow more choice to 14 year olds, more flexibility was needed in Key Stage 4.   There was, though, no clear consensus on the nature of the change required.   I decided to explore this issue further before making recommendations.

5.2   The Interim Report proposed further consultation based on three main options, namely that:

i   the present arrangements (which allow Key Stage 4 students to choose whether to study art and music, to choose to study either history or geography or short courses in both, and to pursue at least short courses in technology and modern foreign languages) should be continued;

ii   the requirement to teach the ten National Curriculum subjects through to age 16 should be reinstated;

iii   the statutory requirement to study some or all of technology, a modern foreign language, history, geography and physical education should be removed so as to allow greater flexibility and wider choice.

The scope allowed by present arrangements

5.3   Various estimates have been given of the proportion of curriculum time which is needed to meet the present statutory requirements.   The picture is clouded by variations in teaching hours from school to school.   However, working from the Department for Education's recommended minimum of 24/25 taught hours per week, the basic statutory commitments, in terms of percentages of available curriculum time, are likely to be broadly as follows:

- English and mathematics (12½% for each subject)   25%

- Science (single subject course)   12½%

  Note: most students follow the recommended double course   *(20%)*

- Technology (single subject or as part of a combined-subject course)   10% or 5%

- Modern foreign language (single subject or as part of a combined-subject course)   10% or 5%

- History and/or geography (single subject or as part of a combined-subject course)   10%

- Physical education   5%

- Religious education   5%

5.4   The total proportion of curriculum time committed to the National Curriculum plus religious education is therefore likely to lie between 67.5% and 85%. Schools which allocate 20% of the available time to science and which also offer a full course in technology and a modern foreign language would have only 15% of the total curriculum time available to provide optional courses which cater for students' specific interests and talents and for other matters such as careers education and guidance.

5.5   In practice, there is somewhat more flexibility available than the preceding paragraph might suggest. The short course options in several subjects can be combined in many different ways. For example, students could follow:

i   technology through the National Curriculum short course extended in various directions, some with a specialist or vocational flavour;

ii   history and geography combined either together or with other subjects;

iii   a modern foreign language in combination with a range of other subjects, including a further language.

5.6   Present arrangements do, therefore, offer some scope for choice. The slimming down of the requirements within subjects at Key Stage 4 could, in itself, extend this scope. The choice is, nevertheless, constrained, partly by the practical management problems that combined-subject syllabuses create for schools and partly by the fact that examinations which attract only a tiny entry may not be economically viable for the examination boards.

Key messages from consultation

5.7 An opinion widely expressed in the consultations which formed the preparation for my Interim Report was that the age of 16 should not be seen as an educational terminus. The argument was, rather, that with so many students staying on to 19, the age of 14 should be seen as the beginning of a distinct phase which runs through to 19, and allows young people to follow courses which lead progressively through from Key Stage 4 to education and training post-16.

5.8 The consultation during the autumn revealed a wide range of opinions on the Key Stage 4 curriculum. The major strands are summarised below.

5.9 A minority of those who commented was broadly content with current arrangements. An equally small number sought a return to the more tightly prescribed breadth of option 2, as described in paragraph 5.2ii. A very large majority sought some relaxation in the statutory requirements. Beyond this point, respondents varied markedly in their preferences.

5.10 Some argued for a statutory curriculum along the lines suggested in my Interim Report (mathematics, English, science and basic IT skills, with at least short courses in design & technology and a modern foreign language). A rather larger proportion thought that this did not go far enough in providing for choice, and favoured a reduction to English, mathematics and science only. This latter view was sometimes linked to proposals envisaging a system of constrained options beyond the core subjects, with students choosing additional subjects from specified curriculum areas, such as the humanities and the creative/aesthetic/practical subjects. Some suggested statutory requirements along these lines, but it was more often argued that balance might be backed by non-statutory guidance, with Office for Standards in Education inspections reviewing the adequacy of each school's curriculum decisions. It has been suggested that this might be further encouraged by a special certificate for those achieving GCSE passes in a defined number of subjects which would include the core subjects. Many recommended the inclusion of a vocational option at this key stage.

5.11 A number of respondents, both at conferences and in writing, expressed reservations about the concept of the short course in National Curriculum subjects. The fundamental concern was that it was difficult in the time available to provide a worthwhile curriculum. Doubt was also expressed about the credibility of these courses to parents and employers. Some argued that better educational value might be obtained from short courses if they were delivered in a more concentrated form - possibly as a unit accredited in suitable fashion. Those who saw potential value in short courses tended to argue that the present requirement to link two short courses together for accreditation purposes militated against the flexibility they were meant to create.

Further considerations

5.12 The raising of educational standards has been a constant theme in the representations that I have received. I quoted, in my Interim Report, evidence from the Adult Literacy and Basic Skills Unit that substantial numbers of young adults do not have the literacy and mathematical skills which they need if they are to function confidently in a rapidly-changing world. Achievement of the National Education and Training Targets will depend heavily on progress in these areas.

5.13 Evidence from formal inspection has shown that the introduction of the National Curriculum has begun to produce improvements in the key subjects of English, mathematics and science. The task now is to ensure that the curriculum in Key Stage 4 enables schools to build on this foundation. The aim must be to equip all young people - and notably those who are currently achieving little success in the core subjects - with the knowledge and skills they need to maximise their potential in adult and working life. The answer will lie, at least in part, in providing courses which engage and motivate the students concerned.

5.14 By age 14, students are developing particular interests and preferences and the curriculum needs to reflect this diversity. Those who are least well served by the current arrangements may, to varying degrees and in different ways, give limited commitment and make poor progress. As a nation, we cannot afford this loss.

5.15 Our aim, therefore, must be to develop an approach to the curriculum in Key Stage 4 which seeks to develop the talents of all students; which recognises the multi-faceted nature of talent; and which accepts that, as a nation, we have for too long had too limited a concept of what constitutes worthwhile achievement.

5.16 Many have suggested to me that, for some students, the introduction at Key Stage 4 of pathways with a more applied approach would increase the incentive to learn and provide a valuable teaching opportunity. In this, there are useful lessons from experience in France, Germany and the Netherlands (see Appendix 3). A small number of schools in this country have seen value in introducing a vocational dimension pre-16. We should draw upon their experience and consider how this aspect of the curriculum might be developed in future.

Broad policy proposed

5.17 We need a framework at Key Stage 4 that encourages schools to provide a curriculum which:

i   continues to develop knowledge and skills in key subject areas;

ii   motivates all students and ensures high expectations;

iii   develops a range of talents and raises standards;

iv   provides recognition of progress and attainment at age 16;

v   keeps open a range of education and training options and promotes progression through to education and training post-16.

5.18 In the light of consultation I have come to the conclusion that it would be desirable to provide somewhat more scope for schools to build a range of options into the curriculum to complement a statutory core of subjects. For very many students, this greater scope for choice would take the form of a selection of GCSEs. Other students would be better served by courses of a more applied character through the programmes overseen by the National Council for Vocational Qualifications as part of a curriculum which retains a significant academic content. This is not to suggest tightly-defined alternative pathways, since many students may find a mixture of academic and applied elements both motivating and crucial to future success. Schools ought to be able to offer a wider range of choice. By extending the range of options to include courses with a substantial element of applied knowledge and skill - the so-called vocational courses - schools will be better able to provide challenge and motivation across the whole range of student aspirations. I recommend this as an approach to be developed for the medium term as part of a wider curriculum.

5.19   I am certain - as, it appears, are almost all of those who have joined the debate - that English, mathematics and science (studied at least at the level of the single award) must remain in the core curriculum for all students to age 16. The position of information technology is less clear. There are those who argue that it should be taught as part of the statutory core. Others, however, think that pupils should have received sufficient instruction in basic information technology skills by the end of Key Stage 3. I recommend that the subject groups generally and the technology group in particular advise the School Curriculum and Assessment Authority (SCAA) on this issue.

5.20   I recommend that all students should, in addition to the core subjects, follow as a minimum a short course in a modern foreign language. We must assume that today's school children may need to pursue part of their career in any part of the world. Britain's economic prosperity will also depend increasingly on our relationships with our trading partners in both Europe and the wider world. It is, moreover, simply not sensible to start a subject at age 11 and drop it at 14. Indeed, I would expect that the majority of students will continue their study of a foreign language as a full subject. But that should be a matter for decision in the school: this recommendation relates to a minimum requirement.

5.21   In the case of technology, as a nation we have a distinguished record in scientific discovery and a proud record among the world's Nobel Prize winners, but we have suffered from an inability to translate scientific discovery into wealth-generating industrial and commercial products. This has weakened the whole economy. We need to develop our commitment to technology, and I recommend, therefore, that technology in the form of a short course should remain as part of the statutory curriculum.

5.22   This recommendation on technology will not meet with universal approval. The fact that the introduction of design & technology has proved intensely difficult in many schools should not, however, lead to a misjudgment about the value of and need for education in this subject. I believe the revised curriculum recommendations from the National Curriculum Council and the further work on these proposals currently being undertaken by the SCAA provide a good way forward.

5.23   We must encourage our young people to develop a fit and healthy lifestyle. I recommend that physical education should remain a statutory requirement, taking about 5% of teaching time in Key Stage 4.

5.24 Religious education and sex education will, of course, remain as statutory requirements.

5.25 History and geography are absorbing and valuable subjects. But I cannot see a reason, either nationally or in terms of the individual student, why these subjects should, as a matter of law, be given priority in this key stage over others, such as the creative arts, a second foreign language, home economics, the classics, religious studies, business studies or economics. I recommend, therefore, that they should be optional in Key Stage 4. In practice, most schools will continue to offer history and geography to those students who wish to study these subjects.

5.26 A majority of students will choose to continue the present practice of studying a modern foreign language as a full course and/or take double science. But those who choose no more than the minimum statutory requirement at Key Stage 4 along the lines I propose would have some 40% of curriculum time available for other studies. Schools would be able to provide a wider range of options, allowing students to pursue courses with distinctive flavours - including an appropriate degree of specialisation - while extending their knowledge and understanding in compulsory subjects.

5.27 These are general recommendations. Specific decisions on choice of pathways and subjects are best left to students, parents and schools. They must, though, be hard, challenging choices. Neither the nation nor our young people can afford soft options. We face a tough world. I urge schools and their governing bodies to ensure that the non-statutory balance of the curriculum is demanding, challenging and motivating. Wherever students' talents allow, they should be using this time predominantly to pursue studies leading to recognised qualifications.

Pathways and bridges

5.28 The advantage of easing the statutory curriculum requirements in Key Stage 4 is that schools will be able to respond to the particular aptitudes and inclinations of their students. It will be possible to meet the needs of different students through broadly identified pathways, which, whilst not exclusive, allow for easily intelligible and coherent progression to post-16 education and training. I set out some of the possibilities in paragraphs 5.30-5.44 below.

5.29 It will, of course, be important to ensure that some bridges are built between emerging pathways. The challenge will be to find ways to allow students to move between pathways, where this is desirable, without undermining the particular identity and integrity of the different courses. Students will clearly need to be offered careers guidance to prepare them for more choice and greater flexibility within Key Stage 4.

The academic pathway

5.30 A pathway will be needed for the very large number of students whose interests and talents lie primarily in academic study. The proposed reduction in statutory requirements would release curriculum time for extra GCSE options to complement or supplement National Curriculum studies. Schools have a great deal of experience in assembling programmes for individual students which allow them to develop specialist interests alongside the core subjects. This is familiar ground and I do not need to map it out.

The vocational pathway

5.31 It will be a particular challenge to establish how a vocational pathway which maintains a broad educational component might be developed at Key Stage 4 over the next few years as part of a 14-19 continuum. As Appendix 3 indicates, such a pathway is already a feature in many European countries, and headteachers and others have clearly indicated their interest in the opportunities which these courses can offer to young people.

5.32 A range of vocational qualifications is currently available for schools to use pre-16 (see Appendix 4). These courses might provide a foundation for progression post-16 to General National Vocational Qualifications (GNVQs) and National Vocational Qualifications (NVQs), in particular, and to A/AS as appropriate. In making selections for the future, schools will need to pay particular attention to the possibilities for progression to post-16 education and training and the public acceptability of the qualifications they offer. The application of the School Curriculum and Assessment Authority's responsibilities for the approval of qualifications for use in Key Stage 4 will provide a mechanism to support this.

5.33 A major new option for the medium term for Key Stage 4 is the GNVQ, which is currently being piloted pre-16 in a number of schools. The GNVQ is designed to offer courses which combine some general education with study of a broad vocational area. It is designed as a middle pathway between academic and occupational (NVQ) provision and is currently available at foundation, intermediate and advanced levels, broadly spanning the standards required for GCSE and A level qualifications. Further details are given in Appendix 4.

5.34   A recent report on GNVQs by the Office for Standards in Education was broadly reassuring about early experience of qualifications on the vocational route at advanced level. It drew attention, however, to the difficulties that teachers have had during the pilot year in establishing the correct standard of work for students studying at intermediate level. Current problems should not detract from the importance of a vocational pathway for some students in the medium term: it will be essential for there to be close cooperation between the School Curriculum and Assessment Authority and the National Council for Vocational Qualifications (NCVQ) so that a high quality GNVQ option can be introduced into schools as an established and well-respected part of the 14-16 curriculum.

5.35   The use of the GNVQ before age 16, however, raises a logistical difficulty. An intermediate or foundation GNVQ is currently expected to take about the same time as four GCSEs - some 40% of the total curriculum time available.

5.36   Given that English, mathematics, single science, physical education, short courses in modern foreign languages and technology plus religious education would require about 60% of the available time, a full GNVQ would leave no time for other subjects.

5.37   There are four possible ways forward, namely to:

i   accept that, unless he/she is a very quick learner, the student would have negligible time for further subjects;

ii   pursue credits towards a GNVQ to be completed post-16. This would certainly be manageable, but may not provide the sense of achievement and consequent motivation for students which a full qualification can bring;

iii   follow a group of specific GNVQ units which would be certificated collectively as a 'Part One' qualification at either intermediate or foundation level and occupy a maximum 20% of curriculum time. This is a possibility currently being developed with the NCVQ. Progression from successful completion of Part One GNVQ, together with specific GCSE achievement, could then allow 'fast track progression' to the next GNVQ level post-16;

iv   discuss with the National Council for Vocational Qualifications (NCVQ) and GCSE bodies how relevant GCSE study and qualifications could count towards a GNVQ, thus easing pressure on the timetable. Many of the schools piloting the full GNVQ are seeking to 'map' courses in this way.

5.38   The approaches at ii, iii and iv above are not mutually exclusive. The last of these would be particularly helpful for a student attracted to a substantial vocational education through a GNVQ and should be explored for the medium term. It is possible, for example, to envisage GCSE work of a suitable standard covering the GNVQ units for information technology, communication and application of number. Further, a modern foreign language might in principle be included in a GNVQ as an optional unit in appropriate vocational areas and some technology could feature within a GNVQ in manufacturing. This would then open up the possibility of providing a full GNVQ pre-16, with time remaining for at least one further subject option.

5.39   I recommend, therefore, that the School Curriculum and Assessment Authority be asked to work closely and urgently with the NCVQ to identify whether such possibilities could be developed.

The occupational pathway

5.40   National Vocational Qualifications (NVQs) develop competence to do a job or a narrow range of jobs. There is a continued anxiety in this country over how much space firmly occupational qualifications should occupy pre-16. As Appendix 3 shows, France, Germany, and the Netherlands already provide this kind of educational experience for a substantial percentage of young people. Further thought should be given to the use of occupational qualifications in this country as part of a more broadly based education.

5.41   Having said this, in the majority of schools, work-related options requiring a smaller commitment of time and less access to technical resources than those required by a full NVQ commitment might be more practicable, at least in the short term. The vocational examining boards already offer a range of provision of this kind (see Appendix 4), and schools will wish to reassess the possibilities in the light of the emerging framework.

Recognising achievement

5.42 The preceding paragraphs touch upon alternative options for recognising achievement when a full vocational or occupational qualification offered by the National Council for Vocational Qualifications (NCVQ) is not being attempted by the student. There is more work to be done here, especially for students who are working below GCSE and GNVQ standards in Key Stage 4. I therefore propose that the School Curriculum and Assessment Authority (SCAA) should keep the needs of these students in mind as the subject Orders are revised, and subsequently work with the NCVQ and the examining bodies to ensure that suitable 'stepping stones' can be created to provide progression and feedback for them.

5.43 I have made recommendations for short courses in modern foreign languages and in technology. One of the possibilities would be recognition through GNVQ units. I recommend that the SCAA should work urgently with the NCVQ to identify the possibilities.

5.44 But many students will prefer to seek recognition of their achievements in short courses through a GCSE qualification. Short courses are not easy for schools to incorporate into timetables, but they do offer an opportunity to engage the interests and abilities of the widest range of students. I believe it will help schools to accommodate such courses, and help their adoption, if the present requirement that a short course has to be combined with another one were abandoned. I so recommend, and also propose that urgent consideration should be given to the general issue of the accreditation of short courses.

Managing the development of the pathways

5.45 If schools are to increase the range of opportunities available at Key Stage 4, resourcing and professional development will need to be carefully managed over time to ensure that the alternative pathways are of equally high quality and that progression routes are assured. Appropriate syllabuses will need to be developed and schools must have access to suitably qualified staff. Support for new courses can come from the kind of joint initiatives with post-16 providers - including colleges of further education - which have been developed, for example, under the Grants for Education Support and Training Scheme and through Technical and Vocational Education Initiative networks. These networks, which will be maintained until 1997, should provide a focus for professional development which can be complemented by the work of the Training and Enterprise Councils and Education/Business Partnerships. It is important that links with all post-16 providers, post-incorporation, are maintained if appropriate progression routes are to be available for all students. I offer these recommendations in the full knowledge that they cannot be for widespread, immediate implementation but as a potentially significant development for the medium term.

Slimming down the content of the curriculum Orders at Key Stage 4

5.46   The content of the curriculum at Key Stage 4 is currently determined both by the Orders for those National Curriculum subjects which have already been introduced and through the syllabuses developed by the external examining bodies in accordance with approved GCSE criteria.

5.47   It is currently possible for the various examining bodies to offer somewhat differing syllabuses, although the extent of this varies from subject to subject. It is relevant to consider whether the scope should be enlarged by reducing the proportion of the content of National Curriculum subjects which is statutorily prescribed. This is a matter to be taken up with the GCSE examining boards as work proceeds on the review of the individual subject Orders.

5.48   The single science course has been criticised during the consultation exercise. This course has, potentially, an important part to play in the development of a more flexible Key Stage 4 curriculum. I recommend that the nature, structure and content of this course be considered as part of the review of the Science Order (see paragraph 4.38).

Recommendations for immediate action: geography, history and technology

5.49   The Government has already announced that the implementation of National Curriculum geography and history in Key Stage 4 should be delayed pending the outcome of this Review. My recommendation that these subjects should no longer be compulsory in Key Stage 4 should, therefore, take immediate effect to end any continuing uncertainty on the part of schools, examining bodies and educational publishers.

5.50   Pending the introduction of the revised curricula in technology in 1996 at Key Stage 4 (1995 at other key stages), I recommend that technology should not be compulsory for students entering Key Stage 4 in 1994 and 1995. This will give schools time to

think through the curricular and resource decisions which the new requirements will
need.

Conclusion

5.51   In summary, I recommend:

i   a reduction in the subjects which all students must study as a matter of law at
     Key Stage 4, with immediate action on geography and history, and no
     requirement on students entering Key Stage 4 in 1994 and 1995 to pursue a
     course in technology pending the introduction of a new curriculum for this
     subject in 1996 in this key stage;

ii   the recognition of the value of introducing the option of a high-quality
     vocational pathway into Key Stage 4;

iii the investigation of how achievement in the minimum mandatory short courses
     in a modern foreign language and technology can be accredited by a range of
     qualifications;

iv   consideration should be given to slimming down the subject Orders themselves
     (where appropriate) to give examining boards more scope to provide a suite
     of challenging examinations designed to test a wide range of aptitudes and
     abilities - academic, practical and vocational;

v   joint work with the National Council for Vocational Qualifications on the
     scope for allowing GCSE evidence to count towards GNVQ attainment with
     particular reference to number, communication skills and information
     technology.

5.52   Taken together in the context of a measured programme for change, these initiatives
        would provide continuing education in subjects which are the gateways to many
        others, as well as fundamentally important in themselves. It also provides an
        increased scope for choice of subjects and educational pathways that will enhance
        motivation for many students who are not getting adequate benefit from school, and
        make for greater coherence in education from 14 through to 19.

6 CHILDREN WITH SPECIAL EDUCATIONAL NEEDS

6.1   Teachers of pupils with special educational needs argue that the National Curriculum must be an entitlement for all pupils. They welcome the breadth and balance it has brought to curricular provision for pupils with special educational needs. It is, however, clear that some aspects of the National Curriculum and its assessment arrangements are not serving a minority of these pupils well. A few pupils who have special needs but who are not formally 'statemented' (that is, have not undergone a statutory process which seeks to identify needs and indicate ways in which these needs can be met) are, for example, expected to work for part of the time on National Curriculum levels which are beyond their abilities. In addition, some pupils who are making modest progress within National Curriculum work are not having that progress fully reflected through current assessment arrangements.

6.2   It is estimated that some 20% of pupils following the National Curriculum will at some time in their school career have special educational needs. For many of these pupils the difficulties will be minor and short-lived. Others will have profound and multiple learning disabilities. Given this range, it is impossible to prescribe a curriculum which will meet the particular needs of every pupil. What the National Curriculum should and must do is to allow teachers and schools to meet the particular needs of pupils with special educational needs in ways which they judge to be relevant. Only when this is the case can we justifiably claim that the National Curriculum is a curriculum for all.

6.3   The majority of teachers of pupils with special educational needs do not want a complex and statutorily prescribed curriculum catering for every conceivable special educational need. A slimmer statutory National Curriculum will, by providing time for use at the teacher's discretion, go a long way towards giving teachers the scope necessary to provide all pupils with a meaningful entitlement to a broad, balanced and relevant curriculum. There are, however, specific steps which need to be taken in order to ensure that the National Curriculum is an entitlement for all pupils.

Curriculum

6.4   As far as the curriculum is concerned, I make the following recommendations.

    i   The full National Curriculum should be available to pupils with special educational needs.

ii   The National Curriculum levels for each key stage are defined in subject Orders. This range of levels should be broadened to include the lower levels at each key stage (that is, level 1 at Key Stage 2 and levels 1 and 2 at Key Stage 3). This will enable pupils who have special educational needs but no statement and who are working below the current prescribed ranges to continue to work at the level appropriate to them without recourse to a statement. It will also mean that statements will no longer need to show modifications to the National Curriculum where older statemented pupils are working at lower levels. But there will continue to be a need to indicate the expected level of performance of the majority of pupils, since it is vital that this Review maintains the rigour of the National Curriculum as it is currently framed.

iii   Work on the revision of the National Curriculum Orders should be advised by a group of teachers of pupils with special educational needs. Each key stage and subject advisory group should include special educational needs specialists reflecting the wide range of special needs, schools and key stages. This will help to ensure that the work takes account of the fact that schools must be able to plan suitably differentiated work for all pupils, and must have time to address other curriculum priorities such as braille reading or the teaching of skills for independent living.

6.5   It is particularly important that children who have been statemented benefit from the support of their parents. In line with legislation, schools should work closely with parents when defining individual curriculum content which addresses breadth, balance and special educational needs.

Assessment

6.6   Pupils with special educational needs can and do make significant progress in terms of their capabilities. Although the steps of progress may be small compared to those of other pupils, they often represent huge progress for individual children.

6.7   At present, where a child of 7 fails to achieve level 1, but has made progress towards level 1, this would be reported at the end of the key stage as 'working towards level 1' or 'W'. Pupils with special educational needs who continue to be unable to achieve level 1 at 11 or 14 will still be assessed as 'W' at key stage after key stage.

Such pupils may have made, in their own terms, significant progress, but there is no way of recognising this other than through the teacher's own daily assessment.

6.8   I recommend that the assessment and recording of achievement by pupils with special educational needs should be reviewed. The School Curriculum and Assessment Authority (SCAA) should investigate ways in which the small steps of progress that pupils with special educational needs make are assessed, recorded and reported positively.

6.9   The recommendations in this Report for enhancing the status and effectiveness of teacher assessment will go some considerable way towards gaining wider acceptance of this as the main means of recognising the achievements of pupils with special educational needs. There has been, however, a significant number of requests from teachers to provide further accreditation of pupils' achievement through non-statutory tests or tasks available to all teachers, which could back up their professional judgement on pupil progression, particularly within level 1.

6.10   Many schools and local education authorities have already produced work in this field and it is important that such work is reviewed and appraised. I propose, therefore, that the SCAA should commission a study of such work. The study will be asked to investigate the effectiveness of various assessment initiatives from the point of view of teachers, pupils and parents. I will ask for recommendations on the way in which any interesting initiatives identified could be made available to schools generally. Such a development would support teachers in their work on accrediting pupils' achievements, and in particular those teachers working with pupils who have profound and multiple learning difficulties.

7.1   The objective is to provide a framework for assessing achievement which:

- offers a clear statement of progression in each National Curriculum subject;

- encourages differentiation of work so that pupils of all abilities are fully stretched;

- provides an easily intelligible means of reporting pupil achievement to parents, teachers and pupils;

- is manageable in the classroom;

- helps to inform parents when deciding on a school for their child;

- helps teachers, parents, governors and society as a whole to assess the achievement of individual schools and the education system generally.

7.2   These objectives point to the need for a framework that is common to all schools and to the assessment of pupil progress against common standards.

The provision of common standards

7.3   Common standards of assessment can be provided by:

- national tests marked to nationally applied standards; and/or

- teacher assessment based on clear statements and exemplar material of what is required at each level and which is subject to appropriate moderation and audit.

7.4   The Government has decided in the light of my Interim Report that there will be slimmed down statutory national tests in the core subjects only for the next three years. It has also accepted my recommendation that, in these subjects, teacher assessment should be reported alongside the test results and that both should be reported to parents.

7.5   For other subjects, the Government has agreed my recommendation that in this period, whether statutory or otherwise, teacher assessment will be the only or main form of assessment. Indeed, it is possible that this may be so beyond the next three years.

7.6   Teacher assessment has, therefore, an important role, and, if the characteristics for a future framework spelt out above are to be satisfied, it needs to be guided by national criteria backed up by examples of the type of pupil work expected at different levels of achievement.

7.7   The provision of national criteria will not in itself guarantee that teachers in different schools are assessing to common standards. The criteria for a process as complex as teaching and learning can never be so precise that, in themselves, they can achieve this critical objective. An effective system of moderated teacher assessment at the end of each key stage is needed to underpin the criteria. But great care must be taken to assess the 'opportunity costs' of any moderation system. We must balance the need for objective scrutiny of the marking standards in individual schools against the very considerable cost in teachers' time that such a system inevitably involves.

7.8   Since teacher assessment in the core subjects is to be reported alongside results from national tests, both systems of assessment should be designed to be complementary and need to be undertaken according to the same criteria.

7.9   It is important to add that this view was not shared by everyone who contributed to the Review. The contrary view is that a criterion based approach to the measurement of pupil achievement is, whatever its theoretical attractions, in practice extremely difficult to deliver. Those who think this believe that it is the misguided attempt to define unambiguous criteria for the complex processes of teaching and learning which explains many of the difficulties teachers have experienced in teaching the National Curriculum, assessing pupil progress and reporting that progress to parents. They argue that the only sensible way forward is to recognise the enormous difficulty (if not impossibility) of the aim; to abandon any attempt to develop objective criteria for the different levels and, instead, to adopt an approach in which the programmes of study define what has to be taught and simple, standardised tests are used to assess pupils' progress.

7.10   I agree that the national tests must be made as simple and straightforward to administer and mark as is consistent with the need to ensure that they are valid, reliable and educationally sound. The mandatory tests this year have been much reduced in terms of pupil time. This has helped reduce the time required to administer and mark them. The School Curriculum and Assessment Authority will, as a matter of urgency, be giving further thought to how the time required for administration and marking can be reduced still further by all appropriate means.

7.11   I do not, however, agree that the attempt to ground teacher assessment in some form of criterion referencing should be abandoned. I share the view of the Office for Standards in Education (OFSTED) in their evidence to the Review that the scale has the potential to contribute further to the raising of standards. Teachers are for the first time judging their pupils' progress against national standards, and they are, on occasion, having to reconsider their assumptions about what can be achieved by children of different ages and abilities. This is not to say that the present National Curriculum criteria (the statements of attainment) are right: it is clear that their apparent precision is sometimes spurious, that they can lead to fragmented teaching and learning, and that they have generated a 'tick-list' approach to assessment which is both burdensome and unproductive. Neither is it wise to suggest that it will be simple to solve these problems. A solution must, however, be found if the improvements described in the recent OFSTED report *National Curriculum Assessment, Recording and Reporting, 1992/93* are to be sustained.

The choices

7.12   The four main options for the ten-level scale and alternative approaches are to:

i   retain the present ten-level scale covering all the National Curriculum subjects except art, music and PE;

ii   modify the ten-level scale in the light of experience so as to minimise its imperfections, and, in particular, to simplify it in the interests of manageability;

iii   abandon the ten-level scale and replace it with end of key stage gradings;

iv   use a modified ten-level scale for subjects in which it is argued that there is most clearly a progressive build up of knowledge and skills, and end of key stage gradings for the others.

The views expressed during consultation

The views of teachers

7.13   The teaching profession in both England and Wales remained as divided as it was in the first stage of consultation: the faults of the ten-level scale are widely recognised, but there is no clear preference for any one of the above options. Some teachers have concluded that, despite the fact that no properly trialled alternative is available, a new approach must be adopted. Others feel that the present scale has advantages (most particularly with regard to encouraging better progression) and that it would be unwise to jettison the huge professional investment made over the last few years. This latter view is more common amongst primary teachers than secondary.

7.14   One conclusion does emerge from the consultation. It is that the issue of the ten-level scale, while very important, is not of the same central significance as the decisions on the curriculum which now need to be taken or the recommendations on testing offered in my Interim Report and accepted by the Government. Just over 30% of schools commenting on the issues arising from the Review chose to raise the ten-level scale issue. Those that did raise it were equally divided between those advocating its retention and those preferring end of key stage gradings or other options.

7.15   The criticisms of the ten-level scale by teachers in the second round of consultation continued to be those summarised in the Interim Report.

7.16   The strength of criticism was such that few teachers believe that the scale should be retained as it is (option 1 in paragraph 7.12 above). Those who felt that it should be kept argued that this was the opportunity to revise the existing model in order to deal with some of its evident imperfections. I do not think that the option merits further discussion.

7.17   The second round of consultation provided an opportunity to consider an outline of the end of key stage option (option 3) and the combined methods option (option 4). Given the fact that nobody had any practical experience of how it would actually work, discussion of the end of key stage alternative was inevitably tentative: the support for it to a degree, perhaps, reflected the strongly felt concerns about problems experienced with the ten-level scale as much as a strong commitment for a different approach. A significant number of teachers advised that the combined approach (option 4) would lead to a two tier curriculum in which the top tier of subjects was assessed through the ten-level scale and the rest through some kind of end of key stage approach. This, it was felt, could undermine the breadth of teaching which the National Curriculum has brought. The decision to confine national tests to the core subjects for the next three years was felt to increase this danger. Concerns have also been expressed about whether a combined approach would be confusing to parents.

The view of specialist bodies

7.18   The former National Curriculum Council (NCC) commissioned a thorough evaluation of the curricula for mathematics and science which recommended (September 1993) the retention of the ten-level scale for these subjects. An evaluation of the National Curriculum assessment of Welsh and Welsh second language commissioned by the former School Examinations and Assessment Council made a similar recommendation. The NCC itself concluded that the scale should be abandoned, but had not at that time developed a properly worked through alternative.

7.19   Consultation with the subject associations has shown a range of views, albeit with most favouring retention of an improved version of the ten-level scale. The Office for Standards in Education argue that the scale should be retained. The teacher associations are divided. Chief Education Officers are similarly split. There were divided views on my advisory group. The GCSE bodies have raised in particular the possibility, as others have done, of ending the scale at age 14. The National Confederation of Parent Teacher Associations advise of a consensus of parents for keeping the ten-level scale while taking carefully into consideration its weaknesses.

7.20   The Curriculum Council for Wales has recommended that the ten-level scale should be retained until a proven alternative emerges and that alternative models should be trialled. The Northern Ireland Curriculum Council advocates retaining the scale.

The three options for further consideration: a detailed discussion

A modified ten-level scale

7.21   The question is: can the existing ten-level scale be improved so that it provides the framework described in paragraph 7.1 above?

7.22   In theory, the scale offers an obvious and straightforward statement of progression. A pupil begins at level one and moves, in so far as his/her ability allows, to level 10.

In practice, there are serious problems with the attempt to define a pupil's increasing mastery of knowledge, understanding and skills in terms of the statements of attainment which characterise the different levels.

7.23   The programmes of study, which have in all subjects (except mathematics) been structured in terms of what it is appropriate to teach pupils at a particular key stage, have proved to be an effective means of setting out the material to be taught. There are, doubtless, ways in which the programmes of study for particular subjects can be improved. Problems with the ordering of material can and should be corrected. Duplication between the programmes of study for different subjects should be removed. There does not seem, however, to be any compelling reason to alter the current approach to the structuring of the programmes of study. Teachers are clear that it is important to have a statement of what should be taught and no plausible alternative to the key stage programme of study has been advanced. Indeed, the end of key stage alternative (discussed below in paragraphs 7.38-7.46) also structures the matters, skills and processes which are to be taught in terms of key stage programmes of study.

7.24   The problem lies, rather, with the attainment targets and statements of attainment. Again, the principle which underpins the current approach is sound: the identification of key elements (the attainment targets) within each subject and the structuring of progression within each attainment target in terms of ten discrete levels ought to facilitate curriculum planning, the matching of work to pupils of different abilities, and the assessment of pupil progress.

7.25   In the event, we have created an over-elaborate system which distorts the nature of the different subjects, which serves to fragment teaching and learning in that teachers are planning work from the statements of attainment, and which has at times reduced the assessment process to a meaningless ticking of myriad boxes.

7.26   It is possible to cut back on this unjustifiable complexity and to improve matters significantly. The number of attainment targets to be taught at Key Stage 1 and 2 can and should be reduced in number and the number and specificity of the statements of attainment should be considered at all key stages.

7.27   A decision to reduce the number of attainment targets at Key Stage 1 and 2 follows logically from the decision to slim down the curriculum in order to focus on the essential knowledge, understanding and skills which must be taught at each key stage.

The reduction would be advantageous in two ways: it eliminates spurious refinement and thus renders the assessment process more credible, and, when combined with a more realistic approach (see paragraph 7.29 below) to the definition of what is required in order to achieve a level, it reduces the number of distinct assessments which the teacher has to make in order to satisfy the requirements of the Order. It will significantly reduce the workload of administration and recording for all teachers and it will provide a more realistic basis for statutory teacher assessment.

7.28 The recent National Curriculum Council proposals for revised curricula for English and design & technology indicate how the number of statements of attainment can be reduced. In English the recommended reduction is from 159 to 83. In technology the reduction is from 117 to 61. The same process could be applied to all subjects as a key element in the slimming down process.

7.29 A simple reduction in the number of statements of attainment may not be the best way to deal with the problems currently being experienced. The opportunity might, rather, be taken to gather the main statements of attainment into clusters to create a more integrated description of what a pupil must know, understand and be able to do at each level. The challenge in producing such 'level descriptors' would be to produce a statement which concentrates attention on the pupil's performance as a whole but which is nevertheless sufficiently sharp and meaningful to help secure reliable assessment across different schools.

7.30 It will not be easy to strike this balance. The job of slimming down must, nonetheless, be done if teachers are to cease feeling as a matter of conscience that they should devote much precious time to the detailed task of assessing pupils' work, recording evidence and reporting progress against a very large number of individual statements of attainment.

7.31 Whilst undertaking the task, the subject advisory groups will be able to iron out some uneven steps between levels and to revisit expectations of what is required at particular levels which have, in practice, proved to be too high or too low.

7.32 It should be possible, therefore, to make significant improvements to the way the ten-level scale articulates progression and to its manageability in the classroom. In addition, the opportunity should be taken through the assessment arrangements to build on recent decisions to sub-divide level 2 in English and mathematics at Key Stage 1 using norm-referencing. This is an important issue at these particular levels because they represent the attainment of a majority of children. A finer grading would be useful to parents and teachers and add to the motivation of the children themselves.

7.33 No clear message has emerged from consultation on whether the scale is proving to be an effective means of reporting pupil achievement to parents. There is considerable scepticism, amongst, in particular, secondary teachers that it will ever become intelligible. But a considerable number of primary teachers report that parents are beginning to find the scale useful. The views expressed by the National Confederation of Parent Teacher Associations encourage persistence in the use of the ten-level scale as a means of reporting pupils' progress in a common national language. A simple numerical statement of the level achieved will never tell parents all they want to know, but, accompanied by verbal comment, it may well be something many parents are coming to appreciate.

7.34 One particular problem with the scale is that parents (and indeed teachers themselves) find it difficult to understand how the level awarded can be divorced from the programme of study which has been studied. 'How', it is asked, 'can the level 3 achieved by the bright 7 year old against the Key Stage 1 Programme of Study be the same thing as the level 3 achieved by the less bright 14 year old against the Key Stage 3 Programme of Study?' One answer to this is that the award of the level relates to conceptual skills and understanding that are independent of the body of knowledge taught within the particular key stage. This is clearly true in mathematics, but, even in a subject such as history where the knowledge element is more important, there is an obvious sense in which the pupil's broader historical understanding can be recognised in terms of a level in a way which knowledge of specific facts cannot.

7.35 Finally, there is the question of whether the scale provides a basis for giving useful information to parents about individual schools (in terms of value-added or simple performance figures), and, more generally, whether it provides a basis for informing society about the progress of the education system as a whole.

7.36 The scale in its basic form does not provide information on fine gradations of achievement. There is, for example, the fact that nearly 70% of pupils achieve level 2 in mathematics at the end of Key Stage 1. But, as stated in paragraph 7.32 above, the School Curriculum and Assessment Authority is already developing finer gradings for this level in English and mathematics so this need not remain a problem.

Teachers can and should amplify the information given by the level number in terms of qualitative comment. In that the numbers of pupils who achieve particular levels in different schools can be compared, a scale does provide a means of informing parents and the community on this aspect of the performance of our schools. The extent to which it can help provide a value-added approach needs further investigation. The School Curriculum and Assessment Authority has already begun this work.

7.37 The conclusion I draw from this discussion is that the scale can be revised so that it provides a better and more manageable framework for teaching and learning. It can offer a statement of progression which will help teachers plan the curriculum and match work to pupils of different abilities. It provides information to parents about their children's progress. It offers relevant information on school performance in both absolute and value-added terms. The judgement as to whether it should be retained hinges on, first, whether any of the remaining options provides a demonstrably better way forward, and, second, on the practicalities of implementing any different approach in the time available.

End of key stage gradings

7.38 The most favoured alternative to the ten-level scale is an approach which is based on key stage programmes of study and end of key stage grading scales. A number of variations to this basic idea have been discussed during consultation. Key features of the approach are as follows.

7.39 The key stage specific programmes of study should:

i make provision for the full range of ability within each key stage, ensuring that the material is sufficiently demanding for the most able as well as making proper provision for the less able and for pupils with special educational needs; and

ii ensure that there is progression through each key stage and from one key stage to the next.

These revised programmes of study should, as far as possible, be based on the content of the existing programmes of study and attainment targets but should be substantially pruned (as with the improved ten-level scale) to reduce the amount prescribed by statute and to eliminate unnecessary overlap between subjects. Careful attention should be paid to their presentation and to the language used in them. There is, it will be noted, no difference between these objectives and those for the programmes of study for the ten-level scale option discussed above.

7.40 The new end of key stage grading scales should:

i   relate clearly to the programmes of study; and

ii state the knowledge, understanding and skills which pupils of different abilities and maturities are expected to have mastered by the end of each key stage by reference to a five point scale, A-E. (Some have suggested a different number of points, but these differences are not significant to an evaluation of the approach.)

It will clearly be essential to avoid replicating the problems teachers have experienced with the present statements of attainment but it will, nevertheless, for the reasons set out in paragraphs 7.6-7.8 above, be necessary to fix at least two points (most probably B and D) by some form of criterion referencing. Grade A would then indicate a performance significantly better than grade B; grade C a performance which lies between B and D; and grade E a performance which falls short of grade D. This approach would ensure that standards were grounded in a firm sense of what is required but would prevent the end of key stage scale becoming bogged down in even greater numbers of statements of attainment than exist at present.

7.41 There is a further point about the relationship between the end of key stage scales and the programmes of study. In the ten-level scale, the level criteria have to relate to different programmes of study. They are and must be less specific than criteria which relate only to one programme of study. The end of key stage scale criteria could, on the other hand, relate to precise aspects of knowledge required by the particular programme of study. This is, arguably, a significant advantage.

7.42 Progression in this approach lies in the development from one key stage to the next of the subject material within the programmes of study. Each new programme of study would build on what has gone before. There is no reason why this cannot be done, and it is difficult to agree with the criticism that any end of key stage model must inevitably undermine the progression fostered by the ten-level scale.

7.43   Potential problems with differentiation affect this approach exactly as they do the key stage related programmes of study of the ten-level scale. Neither approach offers any significant advantage over the other. There is a problem with the end of key stage scale at, in particular, Key Stage 3 in that, if the achievement of all pupils is to be assessed in terms of five grades, then the whole range from level 1 through to level 10 is being covered in half that number of levels. It is hard to see how justice can be done to the progress of either high or low achievers, particularly as pupils move on to the later key stages where the ten levels are particularly valuable in differentiating and recognising achievement. There is, in addition, the point (made at a number of consultation conferences) that, with a small number of levels, the lower achievers may well stay at level 1 throughout their time at school and that this apparent lack of progress is profoundly demotivating.

7.44   The manageability question with regard to both the ten-level scale and this alternative hinges on what is done to the statements of attainment. Assuming that only two grades in the end of key stage scale are criterion referenced and that this criterion referencing amounts to some form of level descriptors (see paragraph 7.29 above), then there is little or no difference between the two approaches. The fact, however, that the alternative approach involves the allocation of one of five grades when only two are defined must raise questions about the reliability of the judgements being made.

7.45   As stated above (paragraphs 7.33-7.34), there is concern whether the ten-level scale makes sense to parents. The end of key stage grading may be more intelligible in that five point scales of this kind have been in use in schools for many years. This approach is not open to the concern that the same level cannot mean the same thing at different key stages.

7.46   There is little, if any, difference between the approaches as a basis for comparing school performance.

Option 4:   the combined approach

7.47   The fourth option is to use the modified ten-level scale for subjects where there is a clear continuum of progression across the key stages, and to assess all other subjects on an end of key stage scale.

7.48   There are two questions to ask about this option: first, is it true that progression in some subjects is in some sense different from progression in others, and, second, will a hybrid approach complicate matters for parents?

7.49   It has been asserted that the subjects which fit most easily into the ten-level scale are English, Welsh, mathematics, science and modern foreign languages. Science is, arguably, the odd subject out, in that progression in the other four subjects is characterised by an increasing mastery of skills. It is this feature which, it is said, allows progression, in theory at least, to be articulated in ten steps. But is it really the case that history, geography and technology cannot be defined in terms of the ten-level scale? These subjects, too, are structured in terms of the mastery of certain key skills and, while it is certainly difficult to 'level' knowledge, it is necessary in constructing any curriculum to decide what it is appropriate to teach to children of different ages: in other words, to 'level' the material which is to be taught. While, moreover, an understanding of, say, any one historical period does not depend on an understanding of any other period, there is no doubt that, in a general sense, the greater the general historical knowledge the richer and better informed the understanding of the particular period.

7.50   It is difficult, therefore, to conclude that there is a compelling justification for the argument that some subjects can be defined in terms of the ten-level scale while others cannot. Some certainly fit the structure better than others, but it is not possible to say more than this. On occasion, moreover, this argument appears little more than a post hoc rationalisation for the wish to preserve the scale for those subjects deemed to be the most important. If this is the motive, then it would be better to state it openly.

7.51   There remains the question of the intelligibility of a hybrid approach to parents. A dual system will be more difficult to understand than a single system. I conclude, therefore, that unless there are compelling reasons to assess some subjects on a ten-level scale and some subjects on an end of key stage scale (and, in my judgement, there are not) we should not adopt this option.

7.52   The situation in art, music and physical education (which are currently assessed in terms of end of key stage statements) needs, however, separate consideration. The initial decision to assess pupil progress in music, art and physical education through end of key stage statements was taken because it was not felt possible (or desirable) to break progress down in these subjects into specific statements of attainment. The system of end of key stage statements should, therefore, be retained for these three subjects whatever the decision taken about the ten-level scale.

Conclusion and recommendations

7.53   We need criteria defining what is meant by a level of achievement in a subject to guide teacher assessment: without criteria, there is no basis for developing local and nationwide standards against which teachers can evaluate learning needs and assess pupil progress.   They also provide a foundation for reporting to parents.   The provision of criteria is common to all three options identified for evaluation: in that sense they are equal.   Turning now to the choice between them, if an approach which combines the ten-level scale with end of key stage scales is rejected, then we must decide whether to revise the ten-level scale or to move to an end of key stage scale.

7.54   It is worth emphasising that much of the work which needs to be done to correct problems with the existing ten-level scale has to be done irrespective of the option chosen.   We must slim down the programmes of study upon which each approach would draw.   We must, similarly, find ways to reduce the number of statements of attainment.   Given that these improvements would be common to each approach, what would be the advantage of moving to the end of key stage scale?

7.55   There is no clear answer to this question.   It is said that the end of key stage scale would be more intelligible to parents and that it would provide finer information about pupils.   The former point may be true: having listened to teachers across the country, the jury, in my view, remains out.   The latter point is probably not true, especially if certain levels (in the core subjects) within the ten-level scale are graded through norm-referenced tests.

7.56   Are there, then, any clear disadvantages to the end of key stage scale?   The disadvantage most often cited is that this approach would undermine progression.   In that the programme of study for each key stage can build on that which has gone before, there is no reason (see paragraph 7.42) why this should necessarily be so. On the other hand, unless there is a clear and explicit link between the criteria used to justify B and D grades in different key stages, progression in learning outcomes is not obvious.   There is a clear attraction in the idea of spelling out what children must know, understand and be able to do as they master a subject.   The aim may, in practice, be difficult to realise, but it does seek to promote a coherent overview through from 5 to 16.   It forces teachers to think about what has already been achieved, and, in particular, it may, in the longer term, do something to ensure better continuity between primary and secondary schools.

7.57   It will be clear from this analysis that we are faced with a difficult judgement. This judgement must, moreover, involve consideration of two important practical questions, namely:

i   Can we be confident that the end of key stage scale would not, in use, begin to produce its own crop of problems?

ii   Linked to this, would a move to this scale prejudice the target date of September 1995 for the implementation of the new Orders?

7.58   If we are not confident that the end of key stage approach will work better than the ten-level scale, then we should not contemplate its introduction. The risk would simply be too great. In weighing this risk two points should be made. First, considerable changes need to be made to the ten-level scale. It is not a simple choice between staying with what is known and a leap into the unknown. Second, in one particular and important respect the work involved in moving to an end of key stage scale is more problematic than that required to improve the existing scale. This is that criteria have to be found to define at least grades B and D of the scale with the clarity and rigour needed if teacher assessment and the tests are to be grounded in a secure sense of what pupils can and cannot do at each grade. To develop such criteria is not an impossible task. But the work has yet to be done, and nobody can, at this point of time, know whether unforeseen difficulties may emerge. We cannot be certain that definition of only two levels is sufficient to enable teachers, on a reliable national basis, to classify achievement into five levels. The alternative of having to define all five levels for each key stage together with the area of overlap between levels in different key stages would be a daunting task. These are material points in coming to a recommendation about the future of the ten-level scale.

7.59   This uncertainty means that a move away from the scale could prejudice the implementation of the new Orders. It may not. The timetable for this introduction (see Section 8 and Appendix 5) is, however, very tight indeed. I regard the task of slimming the curriculum down and freeing up time to be used at the discretion of the teacher as the fundamental outcomes of the Review. This task must be completed quickly in order not to protract debilitating uncertainty. I am, therefore, worried that any additional task could result in further delay.

7.60   To move to the end of key stage scale at this point in time would, therefore, be to run significant risks. I am not convinced that the end of key stage scale provides a demonstrably better way to assess pupil achievement. It has not been thought through in the context of the different National Curriculum Orders and it has not been subject to any practical trialling of the kind the Curriculum Council for Wales says should take place as a preliminary to any move to its use. Conversely, much can be done to alleviate the problems of complexity and prescription that render the ten-level scale as it is currently constructed unworkable in the classroom. Moreover, the consultation has not shown any consensus for change. I give weight to the clear recommendation from the Office for Standards in Education that the ten-level scale should be retained. My conclusion in these circumstances is to minimise the uncertainties. We should devote our energies to an improved version of the ten-level scale as described in paragraphs 7.21-7.37 above.

The GCSE and the ten-level scale at Key Stage 4

7.61   There are, finally, two specific questions which need resolution. Should the decision to assess student achievement at 16 plus through GCSE gradings for 1995 be confirmed for the future, and, linked to this, how should the achievement of students who do not gain a Grade G at GCSE be accredited?

7.62   The GCSE is well established and well understood. There has been too much change in recent years and I see no good reason to upset this understanding. I recommend, therefore, that the decision to maintain the GCSE gradings for 1995 should (with the recently introduced starred grade A to recognise the highest levels of achievement) be confirmed for subsequent years.

7.63   This raises the question of whether the ten-level scale is needed at all in Key Stage 4. It is confusing and unhelpful to have two grading systems in existence. On the other hand, if the scale were to be abandoned, then there would, at present, be no means of accrediting the achievement of students who have not obtained a Grade G at GCSE. Some, moreover, have argued that it is worth giving more thought to the mapping of equivalencies between National Curriculum levels and GCSE grades in order to achieve an objective definition of what GCSE grades actually mean in terms of specific student achievement.

7.64   I do not think that we need the ten-level scale for the majority of students at Key Stage 4. I recommend, therefore, that it should not be used at this key stage. We do, however, need some means of recognising the achievement of less able students who are not able to reach Grade G at GCSE (or its vocational equivalent). I recommend that the School Curriculum and Assessment Authority should investigate, as a matter of urgency, the best means of accrediting the achievement of less able students.

8

THE APPROACH TO REVISING AND IMPLEMENTING THE CURRICULUM

8.1 There was a clear consensus during the consultation that all ten of the National Curriculum Orders should be revised at the same time. The argument was put to me repeatedly that we must ensure that the curriculum at each key stage adds up to a collective whole which is educationally desirable in terms of the overall objectives for the key stage and manageable in the time which it occupies. I accept this and I recommend that the Orders should be revised simultaneously.

8.2 I further recommend that the new Orders should be implemented in September 1995 for all years in Key Stages 1, 2 and 3. I am conscious, in making this recommendation, that concerns have been expressed as to whether the September 1995 implementation date recommended in my Interim Report gives sufficient time for schools to develop new curriculum plans. There is, however, an overwhelming need to relieve teachers of the burden of overload, and, in my judgement, it would be quite wrong to perpetuate the current situation for any teacher longer than is absolutely necessary.

8.3 The feasibility of introducing new arrangements in September 1995 turns on the following considerations:

i   the extent to which the slimmed down statutory material corresponds in content with material in the present curriculum Orders;

ii   the extent to which the structure of the Orders is changed;

iii   the speed with which the new Orders can be drawn up and published, so as to allow up to two terms for school planning depending on the extent of change to the Orders.

Stability of content

8.4 This is central to the decision. The more substantial the changes to the content of the statutory material, the greater the time schools will need to plan for the introduction of the new Orders.

8.5 I have recommended in paragraph 4.36 that the revised attainment targets and programmes of study for English and design & technology proposed by the former National Curriculum Council should form the basis of the review in these subjects. These proposals provide for significant changes to the current Orders. They are, however, already in the public domain and teachers will have adequate time to familiarise themselves with the Secretary of State's final decisions. I do not, therefore, see these revised Orders as a bar to a September 1995 start date, providing that they are not subject to further major change.

The structure of the Orders

8.6 There will be some changes to the structure of the Orders. These are the proposed reduction in the number of attainment targets (especially at Key Stages 1 and 2). There will also be a major reduction and, where it is helpful, a grouping together of the statements of attainment. The objective is, however, to render the Orders easier to implement, and, given that the work is carried through successfully, these changes should facilitate the 1995 introduction date.

The scope for phasing the change

8.7 The elements of the new Orders which have to be taught by statute will almost always be a sub-set of what already exists. This means there is no barrier to teachers continuing to base teaching on the present programmes of study after 1995, providing that their curriculum plans cover the statutory requirements of the new Order. Since it is proposed in Section 4 that, English and design & technology apart, the new Orders should for the most part be a slimmed down version of the existing Orders, schools will have considerable discretion as to how they phase in the introduction of the new Orders. They can, on the one hand, plan immediately to make use of the time which will, in future, be available for teaching outside the National Curriculum or they can, on the other, make no changes at all.

Statutory assessment arrangements for the revised Orders

8.8 Some concerns have been expressed at consultation conferences about whether it will prove possible to develop national tests for 1996 given that the Orders on which the tests are based will be revised. In that the new Orders will be a slimmed down version of the old, there should not, in fact, be a problem: the tests will focus on that which is already being taught. I have recommended minimum change to the core subjects and it is the core subjects which are, of course, tested. I accept that schools cannot be expected to face any uncertainty in these matters. Subject to the provisions of the statutory Orders made by the Secretary of State, the School Curriculum and Assessment Authority (SCAA) must, therefore, provide details of the 1996 tests, with sample materials, at the same time as the revised Orders. It is equally important that regulations on the audit of test marking, on statutory teacher assessment and on reporting requirements are made in good time. Assuming that schools are given this information, I recommend that the programme of national tests should continue uninterrupted into 1996.

GCSE syllabuses

8.9   The GCSE Boards will need time to respond to the opportunities made available to them by any reduction in the statutory content of curriculum Orders, particularly outside the core subjects. It will be the task of the SCAA to prepare subject criteria for the GCSE syllabuses as the work on the revised Orders proceeds, so that the boards have the necessary guidance as soon as possible after the final Orders are published.

8.10   It is desirable that the GCSE bodies have time to consult schools about draft examination syllabuses before settling these. To introduce new GCSE syllabuses in September 1996 following publication of new Orders in January 1995 would involve GCSE bodies and schools following this timetable:

January 1995	New Order published
January 1995	Matching GCSE criteria distributed to boards by the SCAA
June 1995	Draft syllabuses submitted to the SCAA
Early September 1995	The SCAA responds to boards' proposals
Mid October 1995	Boards confirm necessary revisions to meet SCAA concerns
November 1995	Syllabuses approved by the SCAA
January 1996	Printed syllabuses in schools

8.11   This timetable assumes that subject criteria can be settled immediately new Orders are published. It means, moreover, that approved syllabuses may not be in school until

January 1996. This could be a challenging timetable for schools to plan staffing and option systems for the following September.

8.12   Bearing in mind, however, the desirability of resolving uncertainty and getting ahead, I recommend that the School Curriculum and Assessment Authority should hold urgent discussions with the GCSE boards in order to advise Ministers whether September 1996 is a manageable implementation date for the revised Orders in Key Stage 4 and the starting date for new GCSE syllabuses.

9

**TEACHER ASSESSMENT IN THE NON-CORE SUBJECTS
AND VALUE-ADDED**

Introduction

9.1 My Interim Report argued the case for retaining national tests, albeit in a much slimmed down form, in the core subjects. But it also emphasised the importance of teacher assessment (supported by appropriate test material for use on a voluntary basis) as a means of evaluating achievement. My aim was to increase the reliability of teacher assessment and enhance its status in the eyes of parents, teachers and the community at large. I undertook to make recommendations in my final report on the form and timing of teacher assessment in the non-core subjects.

The moderation of teacher assessment

9.2 The Interim Report recommended that projects should be commissioned for developing systems of quality assurance in and across groups of schools. This work has now been put in hand by the School Curriculum and Assessment Authority (SCAA) in liaison with the Office for Standards in Education (OFSTED). At Key Stage 3, where the work has started, consultation has begun on the purposes of and approaches to the moderation of teacher assessment in the core subjects. Following this consultation, the SCAA will be trialling different approaches to moderation through the summer of 1994 with a view to making firm recommendations on future developments. One of the possibilities currently being canvassed is that OFSTED and the Office of Her Majesty's Chief Inspector of Schools in Wales should contribute to the moderation of teacher assessment during their four-yearly inspections of schools (five-yearly in Wales). On the assumption that schools in a locality come together to form groups to moderate their assessments and that these groups are large enough for one school in the group to be inspected each year, this might enable each school in the group to benefit from regular external advice about standards of assessment.

9.3 A major consideration in this work will be the implications of moderation for the use of teachers' time. We must, at all costs, avoid a complex, bureaucratic process which eats into teaching time and involves a great deal of administrative effort. Decisions to be made in the light of the present survey will need to give full weight to this issue.

9.4 The SCAA might itself make a contribution to the moderation of teacher assessment and reduce the time teachers would need to spend in moderation meetings through continuing to produce exemplification material similar to the former School Examinations and Assessment Council's series *Children's/Pupils' Work Assessed*. These series have, on the whole, been well received by schools. They provided examples of pupils' work at different levels, together with a commentary explaining why the work met the requirements of the criteria for the levels. I recommend that the School Curriculum and Assessment Authority (SCAA) should be prepared to continue to develop and publish such material, employing in the short term at least some of the resources that would otherwise have been devoted to the provision of statutory end of key stage tests for the non-core subjects.

9.5   There is also a need to provide high quality standard test and task material which can be used flexibly, and on a voluntary basis, by schools as a means of strengthening their own assessments. Such material would help to ensure that teacher assessment is as standard as possible. The evidence from the Office for Standards in Education suggests that, at least in secondary schools, pupils' progress in most subjects is still measured in substantial part by means of school tests, but that the tests which are used in schools are often of variable value. In the non-core subjects, it would therefore be desirable for the SCAA to develop standard test material in appropriate subjects, or promote its provision by others through a certification process, as an important contribution to the overall assessment of a pupil's work. I therefore recommend that such test material be developed and produced without delay.

Statutory teacher assessment

9.6   In deciding on the form of teacher assessment at the various key stages, two questions need to be resolved:

i   when and in what form statutory end of key stage teacher assessment (that is, recording levels achieved by the pupil in each attainment target) should be introduced (or re-introduced), and in which subjects;

ii   whether there should be any form of statutory moderation of teacher assessment in these subjects, and, if so, what form it might take and when it might be introduced.

9.7   The answers to these questions for the various key stages are suggested below.

Key Stages 1 and 2

9.8   It is essential that there is at least annual reporting to parents, covering all subjects. I recommend that guidance to schools on reporting, based on examples of good reports collected by the Office for Standards in Education, is published as a matter of urgency.

9.9   Statutory teacher assessment would help to ensure that this reporting to parents is based on a set of common standards against which children's progress has been measured. At present this consists of making judgements about the levels reached by children in each attainment target, at the end of the key stage. For Key Stages 1 and 2, it must be remembered that one teacher is usually responsible for covering the whole range of subjects, and that it is often difficult to find ways in which other teachers (or parents) can offer practical support to the class teacher in this task. Any statutory form of assessment which required teachers to make judgements of pupils' progress against all the present attainment targets would make too heavy a demand on the resources of the primary teacher. Until, therefore, action has been taken to reduce the number of attainment targets as recommended in Section 4 and the revision of the National Curriculum Orders has taken place, I recommend no extension of statutory teacher assessment beyond the core subjects. But I recommend that this issue is revisited once the new Orders are in place. This does not mean, of course, that teachers should stop assessing their pupils' progress in the foundation subjects or reporting these assessments to parents. It means only that beyond the core subjects there should continue to be no legal requirement on them to record and report pupils' attainments in the form of levels for each attainment target and for the subject at the end of each key stage.

9.10   There is then the further issue of whether there should be any statutory moderation arrangements in these key stages. At present, audit-moderation takes place for the core subjects at Key Stage 1, covering both the standard tests and tasks and broader teacher-assessment. This audit-moderation is currently managed mainly by Local Education Authorities, which receive funding for the purpose under the Grants for Education Support and Training scheme. Teachers have often found this helpful. An extension of the arrangements to cover teacher assessment in the non-core foundation subjects would, however, require substantial extra resources. Careful evaluation of its benefits needs to be undertaken before it can be justified. I recommend that the School Curriculum and Assessment Authority should conduct such an evaluation and that no decision be made on whether statutory moderation in these subjects should be introduced at Key Stages 1 and 2 until it has taken place.

9.11   Meanwhile, there is the continuing issue of the extent to which teachers need to maintain detailed records of the achievements of their pupils. This has been a particular problem for teachers in primary schools, many of whom have thought it necessary to maintain detailed records against every statement of attainment for each attainment target. Advice, agreed with Her Majesty's Chief Inspectors of Schools for England and Wales, has already been given to all schools that this is not necessary. Further advice, also agreed with the Chief Inspectors, is at Appendix 6, and I commend it for the attention of all primary schools.

Key Stage 3

9.12   Looking to the period beyond 1996, it remains to be decided by the Government whether there should be statutory tests in any or all of the non-core foundation subjects. I continue to think that the immediate priority must be for the School Curriculum and Assessment Authority to develop high quality tests in the core subjects and for those tests to become an accepted part of the assessment arrangements for Key Stage 3. After 1996, it may be right to consider the introduction of tests in other subjects. This is not a decision to be taken now.

9.13   Whatever the decision about the introduction of national tests in the non-core subjects, a reliable assessment of progress and achievement is valuable to pupils, parents and schools in all subjects as a means of providing a clear picture of pupils' current attainment as they look forward to the important period ahead at Key Stage 4 and begin to shape their educational priorities. With specialist teachers being responsible for the various subjects at Key Stage 3, there would not be the same burden of work in statutory teacher assessment as at Key Stages 1 and 2 for the individual teacher. I recommend that as soon as it is feasible after the implementation of the revised Orders, statutory teacher assessment should be introduced or re-introduced in all non-core subjects.

9.14   The question of whether this teacher assessment at Key Stage 3 should be subject to statutory moderation is a more difficult one. Teachers have indicated that, although moderated teacher assessment is desirable, this is an area where manageability becomes a real problem. I have no wish to burden teachers with unnecessary bureaucracy. As indicated in paragraph 9.2, the School Curriculum and Assessment

Authority (SCAA) is currently consulting about how best to moderate teacher assessment at Key Stage 3. I recommend that we should wait until we see the outcome of that consultation and of the trials in the summer of 1994 before deciding whether to introduce statutory moderation procedures.

Special educational needs

9.15 In addition to covering the main levels of attainment of Key Stage 3 pupils, there should also be non-statutory test material appropriate to those pupils with special educational needs of all kinds. The SCAA should explore with outside sources whether there would be interest in the production of such material for endorsement.

Value-added

9.16 The Interim Report recommended that work be put in hand to develop an approach to the assessment of the value-added by individual schools. A working group has been established by the SCAA to carry this work forward with the following terms of reference.

i   To advise on possible approaches to measuring the value added by schools based upon the raw results achieved through National Curriculum tests and tasks at Key Stages 1 to 3 and GCSE results at Key Stage 4.

ii   To consider whether it would be possible to use data from teacher assessment.

iii To advise, as a first priority, on the development of value-added indicators for Key Stage 2 in 1996 from the data available from National Curriculum test and task results and, if possible, from teacher assessment for Key Stage 1 in 1992.

iv   To advise on approaches to value-added that could be used to measure between Key Stage 2 and Key Stage 3 and between Key Stage 3 and Key Stage 4.

v   To consider the extent to which any suggested measures might contribute useful information to parents, governors, teachers, headteachers and Government to complement the information from basic results from tests and from teacher assessment.

vi   To concentrate work on the development of measures based on raw data as set out in (i) above.

vii   To consider, as appropriate, work already undertaken by other agencies in this area.

viii   To produce options and recommendations for the School Curriculum and Assessment Authority.

ix   To provide a report by 30 June 1994.

9.17   The Group's advice will be published.

9.18   It will be noted that these terms of reference do not cover value-added at Key Stage 1. That is an issue that could be pursued to the extent schools choose, as some do, to record children's preparedness when they begin school.

APPENDIX 1

SUMMARY OF INTERIM REPORT AND MINISTERS' RESPONSE

THE INTERIM REPORT

The Interim Report of 23 July made the following recommendations.

The National Curriculum

- The National Curriculum has wide support, has provided breadth and depth to education and is beginning to raise standards. The present nine subjects (ten at secondary level) should be retained for Key Stages 1-3 but the content should be slimmed down.

- Each National Curriculum Order should be revised to divide existing content into a statutory core and optional studies to be covered at the discretion of the teacher. The statutory core of English, mathematics and science should be larger than those of other subjects.

- The number of statements of attainment should be greatly reduced.

- The revision of the Orders should take place within a clear policy framework for each key stage which identifies a margin of time for use at the school's discretion.

- These margins of time should range from 10-15% to 20-25% with the smallest margin being for Key Stage 1 where mastery of the basics is fundamental.

- The time freed up should be used at the discretion of the school to teach optional content outside the statutory core of each subject and for non-National Curriculum work where appropriate (for example, the introduction of a foreign language at Key Stage 2 where the school has relevant expertise).

- Action on changes to the existing Orders for English and technology which were already under review should be delayed so that these Orders could reflect the recommendations emerging from the wider Review.

- The National Curriculum should continue to be available to pupils with special educational needs. Appropriate ways should be found of recognising progress based on realistic expectations of what those with severe learning difficulties can achieve.

- Three key issues should be the subject of further work and consultation during the Autumn:

  o the future shape of the curriculum for 14-16 year-olds;

  o the timetable for slimming down the curriculum: whether streamlining should be introduced in all subjects simultaneously or should be phased; and

○ the grading of pupils' attainments based either on retention of the ten-level scale with improvements or its replacement.

● The existing curriculum should continue in force until the process of reviewing the Orders is complete. The first of the revised Orders should come into force in time for the school year 1995/96.

Assessment

● The purpose of national tests is primarily to provide a summative contribution to the assessment of performance, and any diagnostic or formative elements should be subsidiary to that purpose and should only be included exceptionally where shown to be a cost-effective way of contributing formative information about a pupil.

● The tests in 1994 should be limited to the core subjects and cover only Key Stages 1 and 3. They should be subject to some substantial streamlining:

○ at Key Stage 1, science should be covered by statutory teacher assessment and the pupil time required for formal tests, which should be in English and mathematics only, should be reduced by between 25% and 50% depending on the attainment of the pupil;

○ at Key Stage 3, the pupil time required for the national tests should be reduced from a total of 12½ hours in 1993 to 6¾ hours.

● For Key Stage 2 there should be voluntary national pilots of tests in the core subjects.

● Teacher assessment should have equal standing with national tests in reporting to parents and others by whatever means.

● For the medium term:

○ national tests should be limited for the next three years to the core subjects at Key Stages 1-3;

○ the School Curriculum and Assessment Authority should give priority to providing high quality standard tests in the core subjects.

Administration

● The administration of the National Curriculum and its assessment should be improved through:

○ the removal of unnecessary bureaucracy;

○ simplification and greater clarity;

○ better distribution arrangements;

      o   earlier decisions, and better and earlier advice to schools to allow proper time for planning.

Other issues

- The School Curriculum and Assessment Authority should set up research projects into:

      o   the development of an approach to the assessment of the value added by schools (in collaboration with the Office For Standards in Education);

      o   the development of approaches to quality assurance in schools which might lead to the accreditation of schools for assessment purposes (in collaboration with the Office for Standards in Education and the Department for Education).

THE GOVERNMENT'S RESPONSE

The Government, in its response of 2 August 1993, accepted the Interim Report as the basis for further work. It also announced the following decisions.

The National Curriculum

- The Government would:

      o   retain the existing National Curriculum subjects at ages 5-16 and consider the scope for greater flexibility in the curriculum for 14-16 year-olds;

      o   slim down the curriculum, particularly outside the core subjects;

      o   retain rigorous but streamlined national tests in the core subjects;

      o   improve the administration of the National Curriculum by removing unnecessary bureaucracy.

- The existing curriculum would continue in force in the 1993/94 and 1994/95 school years. Revised Orders for English and technology would not be introduced until the 1995/96 school year.

Assessment in 1994

- The Government accepted the Interim Report recommendations as the basis for assessment in 1994.

Recording, reporting and publication of results

- There would be less form filling and more opportunity for teachers to use their professional skills: it would be left up to teachers to decide how to make and record assessments of pupils' classroom work in English, mathematics and science, with methods of assessment and reporting in other subjects left entirely at teachers' discretion.

- There would be equal treatment for teachers' own assessments and test results: schools would be required to report both to parents and to publish both in school prospectuses and governors' annual reports.

- There would be earlier and better information for schools: schools would receive a leaflet in September describing the 1994 tests and would receive all the further information they needed by October.

- Parents would continue to receive an annual report on their own children, including their assessment results at 7 and 14, and would be able to scrutinise the school's results in its prospectus and governors' annual report.

- In 1993 and 1994 the Secretary of State would publish only national aggregate results of the assessment of 7 and 14 year olds, but those results would not be published school by school in performance tables. GCSE results would continue to be published in school performance tables.

Assessment beyond 1994

- National tests in the basics of reading, writing, spelling, handwriting and arithmetic would continue for 7 year olds alongside teacher assessments of pupils' work in English, mathematics and science. The reporting of results would continue as for 1993/94.

- The first mandatory tests for 11 year olds in English, mathematics and science would take place in summer 1995 following the voluntary national pilot in 1994. Schools would be required to include the results of the 1995 tests in annual reports to parents and to publish school results in prospectuses. National aggregate results only would be published in 1995: primary schools' results in the tests for 11 year-olds would only be included in school performance tables once the tests themselves were established.

- National tests for 14 year-olds would continue in the core subjects. There would also be teacher assessments of pupils' work. Decisions on the introduction of tests in other subjects would only be taken once the underlying curriculum had been slimmed down. The reporting of results would continue as for 1993/94.

Assessment in Key Stage 4

- The GCSE examination would continue to be the main vehicle for assessing 16 year-olds in the National Curriculum subjects. Subject to the outcome of further consultation and consideration of the future of the ten-level scale for grading students' attainments under the National Curriculum, GCSE results would continue to be graded on the A-G scale with a starred A grade for the ablest students.

APPENDIX 2

PROFESSIONAL ORGANISATIONS WHICH RESPONDED TO THE REVIEW

Teacher Associations

Association of Teachers and Lecturers
National Association of Head Teachers
National Association of Schoolmasters/Union of Women Teachers
National Union of Teachers
Professional Association of Teachers
Secondary Heads Association
Undeb Cenedlaethol Yr Athrawon

Governor and Parent Associations

Action for Governors' Information and Training
Institution for School and College Governors
National Association of Governors and Managers
National Confederation of Parent Teacher Associations

Industry

Confederation of British Industry
Construction Industry Training Board
Engineering Council
Industry in Education
Institute of Directors
Institute of Management
Institute of Trading Standards Administration
London Chamber of Commerce
National Food Alliance
Trades Union Congress

Associations of Schools

Association of Welsh Medium Secondary Schools
City Technology Colleges Trust
Standing Advisory Committee for Grant Maintained Schools

Independent Schools Associations

Girls' Schools Association
Headmasters' Conference
Incorporated Association of Preparatory Schools
Independent Schools Association Incorporated
Society of Heads of Independent Schools

Local Education Authority Organisations

Association of County Councils
Association of Metropolitan Authorities
Society of Education Officers

Government Bodies

Curriculum Council for Wales
Department of Employment
Department of Health
National Advisory Council for Education and Training Targets
Northern Ireland Curriculum Council
Office for Standards in Education
Office of Science and Technology
Training, Enterprise and Education Directorate, Department of Employment

Examining Groups and Vocational Awarding Bodies

Business and Technology Education Council
City and Guilds of London Institute
Joint Council for the General Certificate of Secondary Education
Midland Examining Group
National Council for Vocational Qualifications
Northern Examinations and Assessment Board
Royal Society of Arts Examinations Board
Southern Examining Group
University of London Examinations and Assessment Council
Welsh Joint Education Committee

Subject Organisations

Advisers and Inspectors for Careers Education
Association for Language Learning
Association for Science Education
Association for the Teaching of Social Sciences
Association of Advisers and Inspectors in Art and Design
Association of History Teachers in Wales
Association of Mathematics Advisers in Wales
Association of Mathematics Education Tutors
Association of Teachers of Mathematics
British Association for Commercial and Industrial Education
British Association for Local History
British Association of Advisers and Lecturers in Physical Education
British Computer Society
British Ecological Society
British Nutrition Foundation
Campaign for Raising Standards of English
Central Council of Physical Education
Centre for Information on Language Teaching and Research

Centre for Language in Primary Education
Council for British Geography
Council for Education in World Citizenship
Council for Environmental Education
Design and Technology Association
Design Council
Development Education Association
Development Training Advisory Group
Earth Science Teachers' Association
Field Studies Council
Geographical Association
Historical Association
Humanities Association
Incorporated Society of Musicians
Institute of Biology
Institute of Energy
Institute of Home Economics
Institute of Physics
Joint Association of Classical Teachers
Joint Mathematical Council of the United Kingdom
Mathematical Association
Music Advisers National Association
Music Industries Association
National Association for Outdoor Education
National Association for the Teaching of English
National Association of Advisers and Inspectors in Design and Technology
National Association of Advisers for Computers in Education
National Association of Advisers for English in Wales
National Association of Advisers in English
National Association of Advisers of History
National Association of Careers and Guidance Teachers
National Association of Humanities Advisers
National Association of Language Advisers
National Association of Mathematics Advisers
National Association of Teachers of Home Economics and Technology
National Council for Educational Technology
National Council for Mother-Tongue Teaching
National Council for School Sports
National Drama
National Institute for Careers Education and Counselling
National Liaison Group for Co-ordinators of Health and Drugs Education
National Science Advisers and Inspectors Group, Association for Science Education
National Society for Education in Art and Design
Physical Education Association
Politics Association
Royal Geographical Society
Royal Society
Royal Society of Chemistry
School Mathematics Project
Schools' Music Association

Sports Council
Standing Conference on Physical Education
United Kingdom Home Economics Federation

Religious Organisations

Association of Christian Teachers
Catholic Education Service
Catholic Teachers' Federation of England and Wales
Christian Education Movement
Free Church Federal Council
General Synod of the Church of England, Board of Education
Muslim Educational Trust
National Association of Teachers in Further and Higher Education, Religious Studies Section
Professional Council for Religious Education
Religious Education Council of England and Wales

Other National Bodies/Organisations

Adult Literacy and Basic Skills Unit
Advisory Council For the Education of Romany and Other Travellers
Association for All Speech Impaired Children
Association of Assessment Inspectors and Advisers
Association of Educational Psychologists
British Association for Early Childhood Education
British Educational Research Association
British Psychological Society
Campaign for Real Education
Campaign for State Education
Countryside Commission
Education Partners Overseas
Equal Opportunities Commission
General Teaching Council
Library Association
National Association for Able Children in Education
National Association for Gifted Children
National Association for Pastoral Care in Education
National Association for Primary Education
National Association for Special Educational Needs
National Association of Advisory Officers for Special Education
National Association of Educational Inspectors, Advisers and Consultants
National Coordinating Committee on Learning and Assessment
National Forum for Coronary Heart Disease
National Institute of Economic and Social Research
National Primary Centre
Royal National Institute for the Blind and Visual Impairment Education and Welfare
Royal Society for the Protection of Birds
Spastics Society
United Kingdom Association
Worldwide Fund for Nature

Post-16, Further and Higher Education Organisations

Committee of Vice-Chancellors and Principals of the Universities of the United Kingdom
Further Education Funding Council
Further Education Unit
Universities Council for the Education of Teachers

PROVISION FOR 14-16 YEAR OLDS IN MAINLAND EUROPE

1   In most European countries, the compulsory period of education takes place in non-selective schools. Curriculum differentiation is introduced only for the senior classes. In Belgium, for example, the upper secondary curriculum is differentiated into general, technical, vocational and art education aimed primarily at progression either to employment or higher education.

2   In some countries, notably France, Germany and the Netherlands, however, the secondary phase is characterised by different school types which offer education to students according to their capabilities. France offers students a choice of general or vocational schools at ages 13 and 15, whereas Germany and the Netherlands have different ability-related general secondary schools, as well as vocational schools. ·Each system offers, in practice, some flexibility in that there are many connections between the different routes, with opportunities built in for students to change route and destination.

3   Transfer from one pathway to another, however, is dependent upon students attaining the required standards. Some students may be invited to repeat a year or be advised to transfer to a more appropriate course.

4   England has one of the longest periods of compulsory education. England is also unusual in seeing the age of 16 as a significant cut-off point in a student's career. This is not the case in other European countries. By age 16, most students have chosen to follow a curriculum with a general, technical or vocational orientation and are motivated to study well beyond the required period. Unlike their English counterparts, students in Belgium, France, Germany, Italy and the Netherlands select a curriculum rather than a set of single subjects and this approach is reflected in the assessment system. England is exceptional in allowing students to take examinations in an unlimited number of single subjects.

5   In other parts of Europe, it is not thought that the organisation of the curriculum into these different pathways undermines the concept of a broad, balanced curriculum, since a high proportion of general education is provided within each. It is recognised, however, that it will continue to be important to maintain a watchful eye

over curriculum provision to ensure that options remain open to students throughout their development.

6   With this in mind, all curricula within the various pathways have a compulsory core which generally includes languages (mother tongue/foreign), mathematics, science and physical education. Students' aspirations and talents are then met by a range of options which determine the characteristics and orientation of the curriculum. This now enables secondary schools to offer a mixture of general and vocational education and results in a less pronounced division between general and vocational institutions.

7   Developments in the compulsory sector are being reflected in post-compulsory vocational education, with most European countries moving towards more coherent national frameworks, and providing students with broader foundation programmes prior to specialisation.

8   In France, there has been concern to raise the standards of vocational studies by integrating them within a traditional academic framework. In 1985, the French Government introduced legislation to create a vocational Baccalaureate ('Baccalaureate Professionel') to complement the general and technological Baccalaureates. The majority (80%) of students gaining the vocational Baccalaureate are expected to enter employment, whereas the majority (80%) of those gaining the general or technical Baccalaureate are expected to continue their studies. It is envisaged that this reform will be fully in place by 1995. It is worth noting that the number taking the vocational Baccalaureate has increased every year since its introduction.

9   Available evidence from other European countries suggests that the existence of clear curriculum pathways in compulsory education increases levels of motivation and overall attainment, with participation in post-compulsory vocational education and training at a high level in countries where such provision exists in the compulsory sector.

10   There is much evidence from our European neighbours to support the widely expressed view that we should:

        ●   introduce curriculum differentiation at Key Stage 4 in order to raise levels of motivation and attainment;

- ensure sufficient breadth and balance to delay undue specialisation and keep progression routes open;

- involve secondary schools in the provision of technical and vocational education;

- develop vocational qualifications;

- promote parity of esteem between vocational and academic pathways.

Sources

a. EPIC Europe, the link for England, Wales and Northern Ireland to EURYDICE, the official EC education policy information network

b. DFE Statistical Bulletin 1993, International Statistical Comparison of Participation in Education and Training of 16-18 Year Olds

c. Further Education Unit, Vocational Education and Training in Europe: Four Country Study in Four Employment Sectors, 1992

Provision for 14-16 year olds in Europe

COUNTRY	AGES OF COMPULSORY EDUCATION	LENGTH OF COMPULSORY EDUCATION	AGE AT WHICH CHOICE BETWEEN VOCATIONAL AND ACADEMIC PATHWAY IS EXERCISED	CERTIFICATION AT THE END OF COMPULSORY SCHOOLING	FORM OF PROGRESSION BETWEEN COMPULSORY AND POST-COMPULSORY EDUCATION
ENGLAND (present arrangements)	5-16	11	16	unlimited number of single subjects	broad foundation
DENMARK	7-16	9	15	age 15: 11 subjects age 16: 5 more subjects	broad foundation
FRANCE	6-16	10	13 and 15	national certificate	continuation of existing pathways
GERMANY	6-15/16	10	15+	leaving certificates issued according to the type of school	continuation of rudimentary pathways
GREECE	5-14	9	14	single leaving certificate	broad foundation
ITALY	6-14	8	14	single leaving certificate	broad foundation
LUXEMBOURG	5-15	10	12+	completion certificate based on continuous assessment	continuation of existing pathways
NETHERLANDS	4-16	12	13	seven or more subjects	continuation of existing pathways
PORTUGAL	6-15	9	12	continuous and final assessment	continuation of existing pathways
SPAIN (post-reform)	6-16	10	16	single certificate and record of achievement	broad foundation

VOCATIONAL QUALIFICATIONS

'Vocational' GCSEs

1   The GCSE examining boards offer a range of vocationally oriented syllabuses which are approved under section 5 of the Education Reform Act 1988 for use in schools. They cater for students' particular interests and talents and cover a range of areas. Current titles include Technology and Fashion, Technology and Catering, Technology and Business Studies, Travel and Tourism and Key-boarding Applications.

2   Two of the vocational examining boards (the City and Guilds of London Institute and the Royal Society of Arts Examinations Board) also offer a range of vocationally oriented syllabuses which have been approved against the GCSE/Key Stage 4 criteria for technology.

National Vocational Qualifications (NVQs)

3   The NVQ framework comprises 5 levels up to degree and post-graduate equivalent. NVQs attest to competence to do a job (be it at craft or professional level) or a narrow range of jobs. They are unlikely to be widely used in schools so long as students have to be assessed in the workplace or through high quality simulated workplace conditions. Only a limited number of specialist schools may be able to offer such opportunities, either individually or in collaboration with colleges of further education. Where schools consider it appropriate to develop job specific skills, they would be provided within a broader curriculum context.

General National Vocational Qualifications (GNVQs)

4   The GNVQ is designed as a middle pathway between academic and NVQ provision, and is currently available at foundation, intermediate and advanced levels, broadly spanning the standards required by GCSE and A level qualifications. It is possible that GNVQs at higher levels may be introduced in due course.

5   The GNVQ was developed for use post-16 to enable students to explore a broad vocational area in some depth. They are available in a range of vocational areas, including health and social care, leisure and tourism, business, art and design, and

manufacture. Nine other areas are being developed. GNVQs are now being introduced in Key Stage 4 in a limited number of areas.

6   The GNVQ offers a unified vocational course which has clear progression opportunities post-16. It offers flexible teaching and assessment arrangements through modular structures, continuous assessment and the opportunity to re-sit external tests.

7   Foundation GNVQs, which are currently being piloted, consist of 6 vocational units, of which 3 are mandatory and 3 can be chosen from different vocational areas giving students a broader range of experience. These optional units may be selected from the mandatory or optional units for another vocational area, subject to rules of combination and the availability of units at approved centres. There are also 3 mandatory core skill units at this level.

8   An intermediate GNVQ consists of 6 vocational units, of which 4 are mandatory and 2 can be chosen from a list of options within the same vocational area, and 3 mandatory core skill units.

9   A full GNVQ course at foundation level is considered to be equivalent to four Grade D-G GCSEs or an NVQ at level 1. A full GNVQ course at intermediate level is designed to be equivalent to four GCSEs at grades A-C, or an NVQ, level 2. A GNVQ at either level would occupy approximately 40% of the total curriculum at Key Stage 4. The School Curriculum and Assessment Authority is discussing with the National Council for Vocational Qualifications (NCVQ) whether the award of GCSEs in English, mathematics and information technology could be used to justify exemption from the core skill areas or to provide portfolio evidence of achievement in those areas.

10   For students who do not undertake a full GNVQ course, two options are likely to be available, the second of which is under discussion with NCVQ. They can either:

        •   acquire units pre-16 which can be added to those acquired post-16 to form a full qualification; or

        •   once this option is in place, follow an identified group of units (3 mandatory vocational units plus 3 core skill units at intermediate level, or 3 vocational units plus 3 core skill units at foundation level) which are certificated as a

'Part One', occupying 20% of curriculum time. Together with specific GCSE achievement, this could allow 'fast track' progression to the next GNVQ level post-16.

Other vocational awards

11   The City & Guilds of London Institute seeks to provide a framework which links National Curriculum courses and specialist vocational studies as a coherent package through its Diploma of Vocational Education and a Technological Baccalaureate. The latter is currently available in the post-16 sector, but is being proposed for use pre-16. Both schemes would offer a certificate at 16 and include units of GNVQ. The 'Tech Bac' has a heavy technological bias.

12   The Royal Society of Arts Examining Board currently offers Initial Awards as 'stepping stones into full vocational studies'. Initial awards cover areas such as agricultural studies, care, environmental studies, sports and recreation, and travel and tourism. They provide 'taster' opportunities for students who are not yet ready to commit themselves to full scale study of a specific vocational area pre-16.

13   In addition, there is a range of bodies which offer qualifications in basic skills or occupationally specific certification in specialist areas. These courses are often short and can be adapted without undue re-organisation of the timetable. The majority of them do not fit into a clear national framework, however, and schools should review carefully the progression opportunities which they offer, and their credibility with parents and employers.

APPENDIX 5

TIMETABLE FOR REVIEW OF THE CURRICULUM AND PROPOSALS FOR ADVISORY GROUPS

1   To enable the new curriculum to be introduced from September 1995 the timetable for its revision and the associated consultation should be as follows:

1994	Jan-March	The School Curriculum and Assessment Authority (SCAA), advised by key stage and subject advisory groups, prepares proposals for each curriculum subject
	Early April	The SCAA advises the Secretary of State on proposals for consultation
	Early May	Consultation begins
	End of July	Consultation ends
	End of September	The SCAA reports to the Secretary of State with proposals revised in the light of consultation
	End of October	The Secretary of State's final decisions are made
1995	January	Distribution of the new Orders to schools
	September	Implementation of the new Orders in schools.

Advisory groups

2   In drawing up recommendations for new National Curriculum Orders for each subject, the SCAA will be advised by subject and key stage groups.

3   The subject groups will advise on the division of the present programme of study into what must be taught by law and what is left to the discretion of the individual school. They will also advise on the reduction in the number of attainment targets, particularly at Key Stages 1 and 2, and on how the statements of attainment can be reduced in number and reorganised into clusters defining the knowledge, understanding and skill that characterise each level.

4   The key stage groups will advise:

      i   on the overall aims and objectives for each key stage;

      ii   the subject groups on an overall approach to their work so as to ensure a coherent curriculum at each key stage;

      iii   within the broad framework of the recommendations in this Report, on the time that should be available for each subject;

      iv   how to eliminate unhelpful duplication between curriculum requirements in different subjects;

      v   on whether the proposed statutory cores of the subjects when taken together leave the margin of time proposed in this Report for use at the discretion of schools;

      vi   on bringing together the material for Key Stages 1 and 2 into self-contained key stage documents written in a way designed to help the class teacher.

Membership

5   Teachers and headteachers will comprise at least half the membership of the advisory groups. The membership will include representatives of the Office for Standards in Education and an assessor from the Department for Education. The Key Stage 4 Group will include a representative of the National Council for Vocational Qualifications, members with examining and vocational educational experience, and representatives of sixth form colleges and colleges of further education.

6   The work of the groups will be overseen by a committee of the School Curriculum and Assessment Authority (SCAA) and a member of the Authority will be a member of all advisory groups.

7   The SCAA will work closely with the Curriculum Council for Wales (CCW), particularly in those subjects where the Orders are common to England and Wales, and there will be CCW representatives on each of the advisory groups. There will also be close liaison with the key stage and subject advisory groups established by the CCW.

APPENDIX 6

ASSESSING, RECORDING AND REPORTING CHILDREN'S ATTAINMENTS IN KEY STAGES 1 AND 2: FURTHER GUIDANCE FOR SCHOOLS

1   There is no statutory requirement for schools to keep records of teachers' assessments of children's progress against individual statements of attainment. However, as attainment targets currently are made up of separate statements of attainment, many teachers and schools have felt it necessary to develop complex tick-list recording systems. A major influence has been the way that the Key Stage 1 statutory and optional task materials have focused on the individual statements. Many teachers feel that the mechanics of recording teacher assessment information have interfered with teaching and learning. They have expressed a wish for further guidance on what to put in the place of detailed tick-lists and for assurance that a simplified record system would be acceptable to school inspectors. This guidance has been endorsed by the Office for Standards in Education and the Office of Her Majesty's Chief Inspector of Schools in Wales.

2   How teachers record children's progress is a matter for schools to decide and schools may wish to revise their record systems if they are cumbersome and over complex. However, where manageable records have been developed, schools may wish to continue to use them. **There is no point in abandoning workable systems.**

STATUTORY REQUIREMENTS FOR RECORDING

Key Stage 1

3   The Education (National Curriculum) (Assessment Arrangements for the Core Subjects) (Key Stage 1) Order 1993 details **the end of Key Stage 1** requirements for 1994. A teacher assessment for each child in every **core subject** attainment target must be recorded against the ten-level scale. The law does not, however, lay down how children's progress in these attainment targets should be monitored and recorded during the course of the key stage. That is entirely a matter for schools to decide. Schools are required to meet <u>reasonable</u> requests from auditors for <u>samples</u> of children's work arising from the standard tasks and material supporting teacher assessments. There is <u>no</u> requirement to provide this evidence in any particular way <u>nor</u> to provide evidence to substantiate teachers' assessments of every child. The law

governing assessment at the end of Key Stage 1 is set out in Department for Education Circular 11/93.

Key Stage 2

4   Currently there are no statutory requirements for assessment at the end of Key Stage 2. The assessment arrangements in 1994 will take the form of a voluntary national pilot. Teachers are not therefore under any legal obligation to make an assessment of pupils' progress in the core subject attainment targets at the end of the key stage next year. An Order will be made when the assessment arrangements become statutory.

General

5   The Education (School Records) Regulations 1989 require that schools keep a record for each child which includes academic achievements, progress and other skills and abilities. This record must be updated at least once a year. The Regulations do <u>not</u> say how schools should keep the records or make any detailed requirements about their contents.

6   There are **no requirements to keep records in any particular manner** nor to keep records against individual statements of attainment. Also, there is <u>no</u> requirement to keep evidence of the attainments of every pupil in every attainment target.

STATUTORY REQUIREMENTS FOR REPORTING TO PARENTS

7   Schools must give parents a written report of their child's attainments and progress at least once a year. This must include all subjects and activities studied as part of the school curriculum. For children at the end of Key Stage 1, the report must also contain teacher assessment levels of the child's attainment in speaking and listening, reading, writing, spelling, handwriting, mathematics and science alongside test levels in the reading, writing, spelling, handwriting and number attainment targets. Schools are not required to report the results of the voluntary pilot Key Stage 2 tests in 1994. See the Education (Individual Pupils' Achievements) (Information) Regulations 1993 for further details, together with Department for Education Circular 16/93.

DEVELOPING MANAGEABLE RECORDING SYSTEMS

8   It is helpful to define the terms assessment, recording and reporting as they are used in this guidance. **Assessment** is the judgement teachers make about a child's attainment based on knowledge gained through techniques such as observation, questioning, marking pieces of work and testing. **Recording** is teachers making a record of significant attainments to inform curriculum planning and reports to parents or others. It is not possible or sensible to attempt to record all the information collected. Much of it will, necessarily, remain in the teacher's mind. **Reporting** is the process of informing others, including the parents, head teacher, governors, the child's next teacher or school and the child. Records of children's attainments should be useful when preparing these reports. The most manageable systems are those that integrate curriculum planning, assessment, recording and reporting so that each process is not an additional burden.

9   Records should only be kept of significant progress by the child where they are likely to serve a number of the following purposes: informing future planning; informing reports to parents; informing future teachers; and providing evidence for teacher assessments at the end of the key stage. Records should be **useful, manageable** to keep and **easy to interpret**. In particular, there is no need to keep records that are no longer relevant because they have been superseded by the progress of the child. Neither is there a need to write long narrative descriptions of previously known information nor to record the same attainment more than once.

10   Records supplement the teacher's personal and professional knowledge of a child. It is not possible for teachers to record all their knowledge and they should not be tempted to try. Written records complement this professional understanding. If record systems do not provide a significant contribution to teaching and learning there is little point in maintaining them.

Keeping records of observations

11   Although there is no requirement to do so, some teachers have found it useful to keep a note of how individual children are progressing, particularly for those areas of the curriculum that do not produce written work. Some teachers find it helpful to plan to observe each child once a term. This can be achieved by focusing on an individual child or group of children for a short period of time, perhaps a week. It is then possible to ensure that a note is made for each child at some point.

12   Curriculum planning forms part of the recording system because it specifies the curriculum covered, experiences offered and planned learning outcomes. There is no need to repeat this information in another format. Curriculum plans may be passed to the next teacher for reference. If the children transfer to more than one class the plans could be photocopied so that each receiving teacher has a copy. Records of children's progress need to relate only to their individual achievements and not coverage of the curriculum.

Reports to parents

13   Records of children's attainments are likely to contain details that will inform reports to parents. Records that are over-detailed or complex tend to hinder rather than support this task. They should help identify clearly the child's strengths, weaknesses and progress for parents and provide information that will indicate the next steps forward for the child.

14   It is helpful to keep copies of reports to parents. They are an extra source of information for the receiving teacher and add detail to children's individual records. They are particularly useful when children transfer to a new class or school. Previous reports will also enable the teacher to tailor the next report so that it can provide parents with additional information and a clear indication of their child's progress since the last report.

Core subjects

15   Currently, there are different recording and reporting requirements for the core and non-core subjects. Equally, different attainment targets within the core subjects demand different approaches because of their different natures. At the end of the key stage, teachers need to be able to make decisions relatively easily about children's attainment in the core subject attainment targets. It helps to minimise their workload if their judgements are supported by records made throughout the key stage. As a minimum a record should be made annually for each child in all subjects as a basis for reporting to parents.

English, and in Wales, Welsh (as a first language)

16   Most primary schools keep detailed cumulative **reading** records. If these relate to the children's developing achievements in reading and are regularly updated, there is no

need to keep any further records. Records of the title of the book being read and the date will not, however, be sufficient. **Writing** records could consist of one or two samples of work that have been dated; a note made of the context of the activity and the amount of support provided; and assessed against attainment target levels. **Spelling** and **handwriting** will be contained within the writing records. **Speaking and listening** skills require a different approach because they do not often result in work which can be kept. Records could consist of a brief note of any significant progress made as and when appropriate.

Mathematics

17   Work in **number** and **using and applying mathematics** is a central part of teaching and learning in primary schools. Teachers will wish to keep careful records of the children's progress in these attainment targets. If schools use a published scheme, the records of children's progress in number might consist of entries made according to the scheme's recording format plus a more flexible record for other work. Again, note should be taken of any significant progress when it occurs. The **algebra, shape and space**, and **data handling** attainment targets tend to be the focus of mathematics teaching at particular times of the year. Records should be kept of any significant progress as and when it occurs.

Science

18   Like mathematics, science consists of process and knowledge based attainment targets. **Scientific Investigation** will be incorporated into work through the year and significant progress should be recorded as appropriate. The **other attainment targets** will be taught at various times and records can only be made when this takes place.

Samples of children's work

19   There is <u>no</u> requirement to keep samples of work for every child. However, it is useful to keep a <u>small</u> number of samples of work for each child to demonstrate progress and attainment. The samples can also be used as a basis for discussion with parents. It is most helpful if these include evidence of attainment in the core subjects. They should be significant for the individual child by showing progress or best work. The samples can be passed to the next teacher who can review and replace them when they become out of date.

20   It is important to be sure of the rationale for keeping particular samples. The main purpose of individual children's portfolios is to demonstrate progress and inform parents. Large quantities of 'evidence' should not be kept for the sole purpose of substantiating teachers' judgements (see paragraph 25 for further details of audit-moderation).

Non-core subjects

21   Currently, there is no requirement to report National Curriculum levels for the non-core subject attainment targets at the end of the key stage. Therefore, there is no need to organise records for these subjects according to attainment targets, although some schools may find it useful to do so. Alternatively, note can be made of progress in all attainment targets as part of the record for the subject as a whole. Records in these subjects should be flexible and updated when there is significant progress to record. As a minimum, a record must be made for each subject annually as a basis for reporting to parents.

Deciding attainment target levels at the end of a key stage

22   The teacher should feel confident when deciding on an attainment target level at the end of the key stage that it broadly reflects the child's attainment across the statements of attainment as a whole. They need to consider whether the child's attainment corresponds more closely to the statements of attainment <u>as a whole</u> for one level than for another. There should be adequate assessment information to draw on. This includes the teacher's knowledge of the child's attainment that has been built up over time, the child's work, and the teacher's records of the child's attainment described above.

23   Publications such as *Children's Work Assessed* and previous national assessment materials are one possible point of reference when making judgements and they help to promote consistent judgements between teachers. Some local authorities have produced similar materials. These can be supplemented by a school portfolio of work, assessed and agreed by all teachers and possibly with colleagues from other schools.

24   **A school portfolio** contains pieces of work and teachers' observations that have been assessed and agreed by the teachers in the school. It is helpful to include samples that exemplify attainment at each level including the borderlines between levels.

There does not have to be an item included for each statement of attainment. Most schools already have samples that have been assessed collectively at agreement trials or staff meetings and these can form the basis of a portfolio. Once school portfolios are established, it is important to review them regularly.

Audit-moderation

25   The purpose of audit-moderation is to verify the accuracy of the assessment judgements made by the school and promote consistency between schools. Key Stage 1 audit-moderators will wish to see samples of children's work and records illustrating the range of National Curriculum levels in each core subject. An agreed school portfolio of assessed work would be helpful. Audit-moderators will not require samples of work for each child. A system for the verification of schools' results at Key Stage 2 will be established when the end of stage assessment becomes statutory but these have not yet been finalised. The audit system will not require teachers' judgements to be supported by substantial quantities of children's work.

ABBREVIATIONS

CCW	Curriculum Council for Wales
DFE	Department for Education
GCE	General Certificate of Education (Advanced and Advanced Supplementary Levels)
GCSE	General Certificate of Secondary Education
GNVQ	General National Vocational Qualification
NCC	National Curriculum Council (replaced by the SCAA from 1 October 1993)
NCVQ	National Council for Vocational Qualifications
NVQ	National Vocational Qualifications
OFSTED	Office for Standards in Education
SCAA	School Curriculum and Assessment Authority
SEAC	School Examinations and Assessment Council (replaced by the SCAA from 1 October 1993)